Truly Divine

LIGHT ♡ HEART
HANDBOOK AND INSPIRATIONAL CARDS

ROSE TITCHINER

Waterlily Books

WATERLILY BOOKS
PO Box 35
Halesworth
IP19 0WL

Tel: +44 (0)1986 785216

First published in Great Britain
By Waterlily Books 2004
ISBN 0-9530158-1-5

Copyright Permission:
The Gift by Jani King, Light Source Publishing

J. Krishnamurti, The First & Last Freedom pp.41–42
The Krishnamurti Foundation of America

'The Camp Fire Process' from The Journey by Brandon Bays
Reprinted by kind permission of HarperCollins Publishers Ltd
© Brandon Bays 1999

Typeset by T&O Graphics, Bungay, Suffolk

Cover design by Richard Osbourne of BrightstarCreative.com

Line drawings for book by Meraylah Allwood

Card layout, Child's Play card and pink radiant heart
designed by Graham Booker

Paintings for Original Innocence and Living the Dream cards
by Jenny Turner

All photography for cards and book cover by Rose Titchiner

Book printed in Great Britain by Mackays of Chatham, Kent

Cards printed by Carta Mundi

Disclaimer:
This book is a reference work, not intended to treat,
diagnose or prescribe. The information contained herein
is in no way considered a replacement for consultation
with a duly licensed health care professional.

TRULY DIVINE

This book is dedicated to my mother

"To transform the world,

we must begin with ourselves;

and what is important in beginning

with ourselves is the intention.

The intention must be to understand ourselves,

not to leave it to others to transform themselves…

This is our responsibility, yours and mine;

because, however small may be the world we live in,

if we can bring about a radically different

point of view in our daily existence,

then perhaps we shall affect

the world at large."

J Krishnamurti

"Self Knowledge"

from 'The First and Last Freedom'

Contents

TRULY DIVINE

Introduction

I first began working with flower essences thirty-three years ago, and they have been a key part of my life ever since. Alongside the flower essences has run my involvement with spiritual healing over the last twenty-two years, primarily for my own healing and understanding, and later as an integral part of my work with clients.

I began making the Light Heart essences 11 years ago, and since then they have taken me on a profound journey in my own life, and in my understanding and awareness, as I have sought answers to my many questions of: 'why?', 'what is this?', 'what will create healing?', 'how do we embrace all of who we are?', 'who or what are we?', 'what is real?', etc. Sometimes this journey has been extremely challenging – always it has inspired me and stretched my perception of myself, of others, of the world, and of the nature of reality.

This book and cards has come out of my work as an essence maker, and out of my own search for healing and understanding. In this I have been helped and inspired by many. My clients have deepened my understanding of the issues we face, and have prompted me to seek answers to fundamental questions about ourselves and about life.

In the process of making these essences, and understanding the dynamics that they address, I have been challenged to find words to describe things that are sometimes beyond words. I only hope that in some way I have managed to convey the insight and inspiration that I have received and that these descriptions contribute to greater awareness, and greater compassion and self-knowledge. My journey with these essences and these descriptions has been one of increasing joy, peace and empowerment – may yours be too.

How this Book and Card Set Can be Used:

This book and card set has several possible uses:

The book can be opened at random for understanding and inspiration.

You can use the cards & their descriptions together, (as divination cards) to gain insight into many of the issues and challenges in your life.

Each of the cards relates to a description of one of 56 individual Light Heart Essences. The cards can be used as an aide to choosing essences, as well as for meditation on the inspiration of any of these essences.

These descriptions offer greater understanding of oneself, or of the dynamics of a situation. Suggestions are given for possible ways of working with these cards (see page 14), but you can use any of your familiar or favourite card spreads – please experiment and play with these cards!

Those familiar with working with flower essence cards can use the Truly Divine Cards in any of the ways in which they already use flower essence cards. The page number for the corresponding essence description for each card, is shown on the Index Cards in the pack and also on pages 270–271 of the book.

For those who already use flower essences, for flower essence therapists, and for those exploring flower essences for the first time, this book provides a detailed handbook for the Light Heart Essences, giving in depth information on each of the 56 single essences, as well as information on all of the Light Heart combination essences.

Also included is information on: using cards for insight; what are flower essences? how these essences were made; ways of choosing and using essences; combination essences; understanding, forgiveness and the 'Camp Fire Process' a cross-reference index; a reading list; a dowsing chart and useful addresses.

N.B. You do not need to take flower essences or understand anything about them in order to use and enjoy this book and card set!

Using the Cards

The cards that come with this book can be used in many ways, both to gain insight and inspiration from the descriptions in the book, but also as a means of choosing essences, (for those who are interested in working with the Light Heart Flower Essences).

Each card relates to an individual essence description. Each description describes the dynamics of an issue that we may be facing in our life. These descriptions can be read and used on their own for the insight and understanding they offer. They can also be used in conjunction with taking the essences (more information is given on this on pages 218–232). The page number for the corresponding description for each card, is shown on the Index Cards in the pack and also on pages 270–271 of the book.

Each card is a photograph of the actual plants, crystals or elements that each of these essences was made from, with the exception of three cards: Child's Play, Original Innocence and Living the Dream. These three essences, were made solely with light and intention, and artist Jenny Turner, has worked with the inspiration of Original Innocence and Living the Dream to paint two beautiful cards, and Graham Booker designed the magical image for the Child's Play card.

Unlike some divination cards, there are no contrary card descriptions in this book. As our awareness develops, we tend to flip between the positive and negative aspects of issues we are addressing. Therefore, we may gain insight from both the positive and negative aspects of each description.

If you are familiar with working with divination cards you may already have some favourite card layouts that you would like to try with these cards. If not, or if you would like to experiment with some new card spreads, there are some suggestions given overleaf for some you might like to try in different situations. Please feel free to play with these cards, and enjoy!

Before You Begin

Before using these cards please remove any blank cards and index cards from the pack. (The index cards give the page numbers in the book for the individual descriptions relating to each of the cards.)

Shuffle the cards well, making sure that they are all face down.

What you do next is up to individual preference. You can either deal your cards straight from the top, or the bottom of the pack in the order of your card spread, or you can pick the cards at random from different parts of the pack. You can also spread the cards face down in a fan on the floor in front of you, or on a table, and then choose the individual cards that you feel drawn to. When you have picked the card or cards for your card spread, turn them over one by one, and read their descriptions in the book.

Sometimes the whole of a description will talk to you, and will feel completely relevant to your current situation. At other times, just one aspect of a description will relate to the issues you are addressing. If you are particularly moved by a card spread, you can leave these cards on your table for a day or so, as a focus, to remind you of the dynamics you are dealing with, and the healing and understanding that you are trying to embrace.

Truly Divine Card Spreads

Before you choose your cards, hold in your awareness the issue that you want help or guidance with, and as you pick each card, focus on the aspect or dynamic that that card will relate to.

Card for Today

This is a quickie:

One card for today, to help with your work, with a current situation, as a theme for today, or as a support for your inner child.

A Helping Hand

Another quick spread, to offer support and guidance in any situation:

Card no.1:

This card helps us to understand the challenge of a situation.

Card no.2:

This card brings a personal message of support from the angels and from our friends in spirit, to help us with this situation.

Reunion

For whenever we feel conflicted, divided, or torn between head and heart:

Card no.1:

Pick this card with the right hand. This card relates to the left side of our brain – the logical, literal, and linear side of our brain, and to what our masculine aspect wants, needs, or is challenged by.

Card no.2:

Pick this card with the left hand. This card relates to the right side of our brain – to the lateral, intuitive, visionary, expansive side of our brain, and to what our feminine aspect wants, needs or is challenged by.

Card no.3:

Pick this card with both hands. This card shows us what will unite and integrate the two aspects of our awareness in this situation, so that we can move forward in balance and harmony.

The Eagle

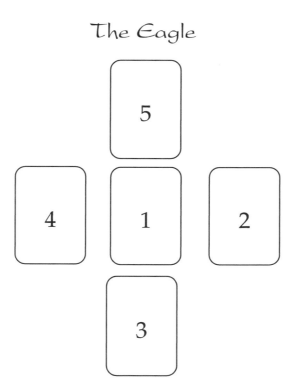

For whenever we need to get a clear understanding of the dynamics of a relationship or a group situation:

Card no.1:

This card represents our own personal challenge and our opportunity for learning, within the relationship or the group at this time.

Card no.2:

This card relates to the emotional or energetic dynamics of the other, or others, in this relationship or group. It may indicate their challenge or their emotional wound and how it affects this situation.

Card no.3:

This card relates to the challenge or wound shared by all parties in this situation.

Card no.4:

This card relates to the positive contribution that we can make towards the dynamics of this situation.

Card no.5:

This card is like the eagle's eye. It shows the higher purpose and the greater potential for healing for all involved in this situation. It indicates how the dynamics of a situation may change, particularly if we grasp our own personal healing opportunity within the relationship or the group, at this time.

The Dreamcatcher

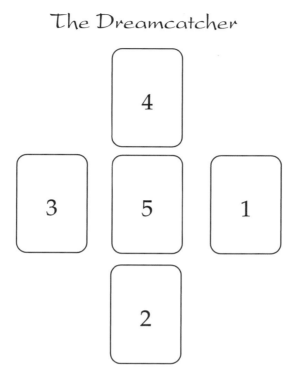

For when we wish to focus on our personal vision for ourselves,

and how we might realise that vision:

Card no.1:

This card represents our personal vision for ourselves.

Card no.2:

This card represents our challenge in integrating and manifesting our vision in the world.

Card no.3:

This card shows us what will inspire us in realising our dream – where our spiritual and creative inspiration lies.

Card no.4:

This card shows us the higher purpose of our dream at this time – our soul incarnation choice.

Card no.5:

This card shows us our heart's deepest longing in our vision for ourselves.

The Dreamcatcher's Tails: In addition to the above cards we may wish to pick up to three more cards to place beneath the dreamcatcher, to bring messages from our spirit guides, offering support and guidance with any further specific or general questions, we have about our dream for ourselves.

Heart Family

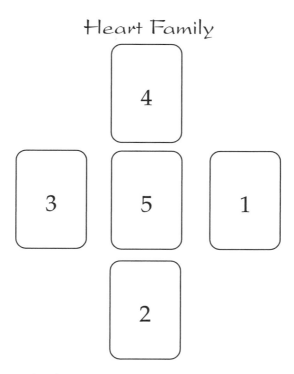

This card spread is for our inner child, for when we need support, and for when we need to know that we are not alone:

Card no.1:

This card indicates the challenge that our inner child is facing at the moment.

Card no.2:

This card brings a personal message from the divine mother.

Card no.3:

This card brings a personal message from the divine father.

Card no.4:

This card brings a personal message from our spiritual companions, our brothers and sisters in spirit.

Card no.5:

This card brings a personal message from the Grandparents, the Elders or the Ancestors.

At the Heart of Being

energy signature of the heart of sacred Oak – ("The Timeless One")

Indications: for whenever we seek outside ourselves for wisdom, love, worth, strength, security, abundance or happiness; for deep lack of self-worth or self confidence; for when we are disturbed by events around us or by the reactions of others towards us; for the heart and base chakras

❄

For Coming Home to the wholeness of our being; for being deeply rooted within our timeless core self – in the infinite peace of our being – remaining centred and undisturbed, even when all around us is turmoil and change; knowing that nothing can affect our essential being and knowing that we can return to, and remain in, our wholeness at all times. At the Heart of Being can be used to help us to come to a point of stillness and connection when meditating or seeking attunement and guidance. (see At One combination).

At the Heart of Being reminds us that all that we seek lies within us in the core of our being, which remains whole and at peace regardless of the passage of time, or the passing of worlds, or of people. It says that we lack nothing, and that our sense of lack, whether of peace, love, wisdom, worth, abundance or joy – is only in our perception. It reminds us that whenever we experience pain and suffering it is because we have moved out of our wholeness – out of the center of our being and have separated ourselves from our unalterable perfection and light – from our love.

The purpose of this essence is to bring us home to ourselves, to re-unite us with ourselves.It encourages us to settle once more into the wholeness of our being – to seek no more – and to know that we lack nothing, and that nothing can diminish us or be taken away from us. It inspires us to find our point of reference within ourselves – to seek resources, guidance and succour within, in communion with our guides and our divine being, so that we need no longer need outside opinion, support or approval.

Traditionally the oak has been associated with strength, endurance, courage and protection. In the Celtic Ogham it's name is 'Duir' or 'Dwr', meaning door, which refers to its association as a doorway to inner strength and spirituality, The oak is often very long lived and can survive many centuries. (source – "The Sacred Tree" by Glennie Kindred)

See also: One Being, Reunion, Comfrey, Sweet Hunza, Sky Blue Comfrey.

Beauty in the Eye

Orchid – Phalaenopsis hybrid

"Beauty is in the eye of the beholder"

– Margaret Wolfe Hungerford

Indications: for whenever we are holding back at some level from embracing someone or something: for dissatisfaction, yearning for 'better' things or grieving over unrealised dreams; for when we cut ourselves off from others or from life because of arrogance or prejudicial judgements; for when we are dissatisfied with ourselves, with our progress, our achievements, or with our appearance; for when we need to recognise the difference between real and illusory dreams; for the brow and heart chakras

❉

Beauty in the Eye dissolves the scales from our heart and eyes, enabling us to see the true beauty of people and things with discernment and without prejudice or pre-conceived judgement. It encourages us to look past external appearances to the beauty that lies within – particularly with people, situations or things that we may have perceived as mundane, over familiar, unglamorous, boring, perhaps even ugly, repulsive, or in some way not good enough for us.

There are times when we close our heart and eyes and do not see the beauty, richness and teaching that stands right in front of us, that lives with us, walks with us, or that we pass each day. When we find ourselves holding back from fully embracing somebody or something, Beauty in the Eye enables us to discern whether we need to embrace a

27

situation more fully, or whether it would fulfil the most loving purpose for all, for us to move on.

When we are dissatisfied and yearning for 'greener grass', a 'better' life, a 'better' partner, home, job, or work companions, or when we are grieving over unrealised dreams, Beauty in the Eye makes clear the difference between our real and illusory dreams and shows us what it is that we need to embrace and what we need to change or to move on from. When we need to dive deeper into our present experience this essence reveals to us the beauty, richness and teaching within our immediate environment. If we need to move on it brings clarity, peace and directed action.

Beauty in the Eye dissolves our prejudicial perceptions, preconceived judgements and arrogance. It opens our hearts and eyes to embrace wholeheartedly the divine perfection of the people, things and experiences that make up our lives. It shows us that those people and things that we find most hard to embrace in our lives mirror back to us the very deep fears and judgements we have about ourselves – those parts of ourselves that we are least willing to embrace and that we fight hard to bury or eradicate. Beauty in the Eye encourages us to wholeheartedly embrace and love our essential humanness – our foibles, habits, weaknesses and 'imperfections', and within that loving embrace a wondrous and magical alchemy occurs as our true beauty is revealed to us.

(Note: This orchid was given to me by a friend – I had long wanted to have an orchid, and although I was excited and felt really gifted to be given one, I was also disappointed because I didn't immediately like the appearance of this orchid and felt that it would not have been one I would have chosen for myself. Interestingly, it had also been given to my friend and she herself had found it unattractive and had thought that I might appreciate it more than her. I have since become overwhelmed by the beauty of this orchid!)

See also: Yellow Hyacinth, Pink Cherry, Blue Salvia, Original Innocence and Phoenix Rebirth

Bluebell Grove

Environmental essence of Bluebell Grove

Indications: for exhaustion, stress, burn out; feeling overwhelmed by responsibility; for when we need to stop thinking and trying to solve things with our mind; for when we need to take time out to re-connect with ourselves, with stillness and with nature.

Connection to the energy of the healing grove; for creating for ourselves the time and space for deep peace, relaxation, rest and renewal; for whenever we need to take time out from doing, to restore our energy and to re-inspire our soul.

Bluebell Grove helps us connect to the deep peace and stillness of our being. It reminds us that we have within us at all times an oasis of stillness and peace into which we can relax deeply whenever we need to take the time to rest and restore our body, mind and spirit. Bluebell Grove can be used to enhance meditation and relaxation. It encourages us to put aside our cares and responsibilities and to settle deeply into the inner sanctuary and peace of our being.

Drawing on the inspiration of Bluebell Grove we become able to relax and meditate more deeply and it becomes easier to approach our whole life as a living meditation.

See also: Cyclamen, At the Heart of Being, One Being, Pussy Willow, Grandmother's Arms, Rosebay Willowherb, Green Alexanders and Living the Dream.

Blue Delphinium

Delphinium sp.

Indications: fear of speaking out and speaking one's truth; for releasing inhibitions related to speaking, singing, writing and listening; for developing the ability to listen, both to others and within, for listening within for the words to say and for when and how to communicate; for listening to the voice of our inner heart; for the throat and heart chakras.

Most of us have a blockage at some level in relation to speaking out, and some degree of fear about what will happen when we open our mouths to speak our truth. This fear often has its root in past experiences where we may have suffered as a result of speaking out, or where our own lives or the lives of others would have been put at risk if we had dared to speak out.

There are often cultural or political requirements in different societies, to be polite or politically correct, or powerful sanctions taken against those who voice anti government or controversial opinions. As we come into our full expression we encounter many opportunities to release long held patterns of fear and suppression. The voice of truth and love is liberating for all – it breaks the patterns of anger, denial, judgement and shame, freeing our hearts so that love may flow.

If we have never learnt how to communicate effectively in a way that can be heard, we may feel a sense of hopelessness in relation to speaking out – an "Oh what's the point – it never works when I open my mouth – it's safer to say nothing and to just get on with my life". This leads to a sense of hopelessness, a lack of honesty and to a repeated suppression of anger and frustration.

Blue Delphinium gives us the courage to speak out (particularly when used in combination with Inner Fire, Goldenrod, Physostegia and Red Poppy or Phoenix Rebirth). It encourages us to stay calm and centred whilst listening and speaking, and it helps us to know when to speak and when to be silent. Effective communication is as much about listening as it is about speaking. If we listen to what others are saying, both verbally and through their body language and energy and if we listen within for the words to say and for the timing of when to say it – then we connect to truth, so that our communication can best be expressed and heard.

Blue Delphinium inspires us to communicate from a peaceful inner core of worthiness – knowing that we are all equal, with an equal right to govern our lives, and to speak and express what is true for each of us. It highlights where our fears lie in relation to speaking out and it encourages us to let go these fears and these feelings of powerlessness, calming our hearts – to become at peace with our own authority and truth.

The power of the spoken word is immense – and even more so, the energy and intention that lies behind what we say. Sometimes we fear the waves created when we speak the truth and it is this fear of other people's reaction and judgements that prevents us from speaking out. Blue Delphinium clarifies the intention of our heart, inspiring us to seek to bring clarity through our words, and to realise that we have the ability to create love and healing through what we choose to say and how and when we say it.

There are times when we are unable to say what we feel to someone, either because that person is too reactive and defended and therefore would be unable to hear what we have to say, or because it is not possible to speak to them – they may have died or they may be unavailable. Sometimes we may have held down our anger and suppressed our feelings over a long period of time. Many of us have an energetic block or a resistance between our heart and throat chakras as a result of holding back all that we have been afraid to say, or have been unable to say.

In order to heal and let go we do actually need to move this energy out through our throat chakra, by voicing aloud how we feel. If we can't do this directly to the person or people concerned, we need to find another way to talk with them, to bring our feelings out into the open – to express them verbally out loud, and to understand the reality of the situation for both parties. One of the most effective ways to do this in a 'Camp Fire Process', such as the one used by Brandon Bays in her Journey work (See Useful Addresses). This process of voicing long held in feelings can create a profound turning point in our healing journey. Blue Delphinium, Heart Flow and Phoenix Rebirth can also assist with this process. (The 'Camp Fire Process' is reproduced in this book on pages 233–238).

Part of the problem for many of us is that we have not been taught how to communicate effectively. We have not learnt how to say things in a way that can be heard, that is non-threatening, non-judgemental, straightforward, honest, and peacefully assertive. We may have been brought up in a family where one did not say what one really felt, where one was expected to be polite and courteous, where anger was taboo and where angry outbursts were crushed. Or we may have been brought up in a family where angry outbursts and arguments were the norm. Either way we would not have learnt effective communication and listening skills!

In order for our voice to be heard we need to use language that does not judge or blame. Ineffective communication calls names, blames, judges and dumps personal issues on others. When someone talks to us in this way we either stop listening, or react defensively.

Good communication skills are particularly important when trying to address sensitive issues with others. We need to own our part in a situation and we need to own our own feelings about what is, or was, going on. Blue Delphinium helps us to listen within to how we feel, for the words to say and for the tone of voice to use. It also helps us to listen for the most appropriate time to speak. It encourages us to listen more intently to what others are saying, not only to the words they are saying but also to the levels of unspoken communication that are occurring.

When we are writing, Blue Delphinium helps us to listen within for the words to express what it is that we wish to say. When singing, Blue Delphinium, combined with Heart Flow and Celandine helps us to let go our anxiety about performance, and our inhibitions about being heard by others. It also helps us to listen more intently for the notes to sing and for the timing of the words and the notes.

Blue Delphinium can be used on it's own as a diagnostic tool whenever we find ourselves in emotional turmoil but cannot identify the true reason for our distress. It helps us to get in touch with our inner voice – the voice of our heart, so that we can begin to understand what lies at the root of our pain. Once we can see clearly what we are dealing with, we can begin to find ways to heal and to transform.

This essence was taken over several months by a seven year old boy with Aspergers Syndrome who had been unable to understand anything other than the literal meaning of the words that people spoke. He didn't understand common turns of phrases, jokes, innuendo or sarcasm. He could not understand and was unwilling to join in any fantasy or imaginary games. He was also very reluctant to speak in public, saying that his voice was too deep.

Within a few months of continually taking Blue Delphinium in combination with Child's Play and Reunion he became able to understand the subtler levels of what was being communicated by those around him. He began to understand jokes, developed his own sense of humour, started making up stories and poems and was able to join in imaginary games, with great involvement and gusto. His mother and teachers commented that he had 'found his voice', was becoming chatty and had lost his fear of talking to other children. He was obviously now thinking about effective ways to communicate with others and was able to describe complex situations and his feelings about them. He later went on to recite a poem in front of a large audience at a public speaking competition. He received an award for his expressive and warm rendition. A few weeks later, he sang a solo rock song into a microphone, at the school's nativity play. He really 'went for it' – it was amazing to see.

See also: Goldenrod, Red Poppy, Inner Fire, Physostegia, Phoenix Rebirth, Pink Cherry, Heart Flow, Celandine, Red Quince, At the Heart of Being

Blue Salvia

Salvia guarantica "Blue Enigma"

Indications: for whenever we are confused and can't see clearly what is really going on in a situation; for when we sense that things are not as they might appear; for when we sense that there is a hidden agenda; for when we can see clearly the truth in a situation but lose confidence in our vision because this view is not upheld by others; for when our thinking is muddled and slow.

❄

Blue Salvia helps us to see clearly through confusion and illusion, to uncover what is hidden. It enables us to discern with love and without judgement, the truth behind a mask or smokescreen. If we find ourselves in a situation in which we do not understand what is really going on, particularly if we sense that all is not as it appears, Blue Salvia helps us to see with love, whatever lies behind our own personal confusion about ourselves, as well as to see clearly what is really going on with another person or a situation. It can bring greater clarity when something seems to be an enigma or puzzling, and when we receive mixed messages and need to understand what is real.

Blue Salvia also relates to those children who see and understand very clearly the dynamics of what is happening around them, and in the world. Those that they come into contact with can feel quite threatened by this, particularly since these children have the ability to pinpoint emotional wounds and hypocrisy very accurately, and often do so in a very direct and unequivocal way. Those around them, in an attempt to protect themselves from this exposure, may turn on the child, denying the child's vision, and criticising or ridiculing them. Sometimes this leads to the child suppressing what they see since it causes them so much trouble – or in their becoming confused since they feel that their vision is wrong in some way, because it is not recognised or confirmed by those around them.

Adults can struggle in the same way, because we too may see clearly what is going on around us in the world, and may feel isolated if others do not share our understanding or vision. Blue Salvia helps us to discern the reality of a situation, with greater clarity, with love, and without judgement. It supports us in valuing to ourselves, the clarity of our vision, so that we do not undermine ourselves, and do not deny or lose sight of our understanding, even when the rest of the world does not agree with our vision. It helps us to honour our vision, even if it is something that we might have to hold inside ourselves and never share with others. Blue Salvia can also highlight where we are deceiving ourselves about our own dynamics, or about the dynamics of others or of the world.

Where we have difficulty communicating our vision to others in a way that can be heard, we may need to combine the inspiration of Blue Salvia with Blue Delphinium, to encourage us to listen inside for an appropriate time to say what it is that we wish to say, and to listen for the words to say, in order that our what we say can best be heard and understood.

When I had written up this essence after I had made it, I was trying to find the name of the plant. It was a plant that I had brought from my mother's garden and I was sure that it had a plant label attached to the base of the stem. I pulled away the undergrowth surrounding the base of this tall plant and found a mud-smeared label – which when cleaned revealed its name – 'Salvia guarantica – "Blue Enigma" '. When something like this happens I feel very supported and grateful for the confirmation of what I have seen, because sometimes I have wondered who I'm kidding – but less and less now because of these unexpected moments of confirmation. It was interesting that the plant chose to support what I had seen, and that this is the role of this essence – to confirm what we know and see on a hidden level.

See also: Goldenrod, Yellow Hyacinth, Physostegia, Pink Cherry, Beauty in the Eye, Cherry Plum Fruit, Comfrey, Honesty, True Power, Violet, Peaceful Detachment, Sweet Hunza, Sweet Pea, Father Sun, Pure Love, Inner Fire, At the Heart of Being.

Celandine

Ranunculus ficarius

Indications: depression; pessimism; gloominess; negativity; S.A.D.; for grumbling, discontented 'Eeyore' days; for whenever we are continually critical or 'nitpicking'; for whenever we need the inspiration of light and joy; for loss of trust in goodness; for when we have a tendency to gossip or to spread gloom and negativity in our conversations; for the crown and solar plexus chakras

Whenever we are depressed, world weary and have lost our ability to feel and express joy and appreciation, Celandine helps to lift our spirits, inspiring us to look again, to see the wonder, beauty and magic of our world and to express that appreciation in our lives.

Sometimes we can get into a habit of looking negatively at the world, or at others – as though we have put on dark glasses, and are looking for the worst, or are looking at what's not right, rather than enjoying what's right and good in our own lives, and in the world. We may be critical or nit-picking – our criticism or negativity spreading a damper on other people's joy or achievement.

Celandine helps us to focus on the good in our lives and in the world, and it opens our eyes to how we can bring joy and goodness through our own actions, and through our enjoyment and appreciation of life.

When we have allowed our life to be driven by fear and deep levels of stress, the inspiration of Celandine lightens and brings joy to the heart and solar plexus. It encourages us to look at the world with less jaundiced eyes, to examine the way we see things and the way that we create our reality by our choices, thoughts and words.

Celandine reminds us that we can choose to perceive the world through the dark glasses of negativity or we can embrace the wonder of life and the immense power that we have to create a life that expresses joy and love. Is our cup empty or full? Are we powerless or powerful?

Celandine invites us to look at the power of what we think and say. If someone asks us how we are and how things are, do we confirm and join in negative outlooks on situations or on life in general? Do we express gloom and doom? What kind of agreements do we enter into with others when we talk to them about life? Do we join in confirming a reality of love, joy and empowerment or do we confirm a negative view of ourselves and of life?

Celandine doesn't ask us to deny how we are feeling. It simply inspires us to look at things afresh, to see the gifts in our life and in our experience. It encourages us to see whether things really are as bad as we have allowed ourselves to think or to describe to others – or whether we can in fact allow the light of joy to shine through our lives – to enlighten our own experience and perhaps also that of others.

See also: Blue Delphinium, Golden Blessings, Living the Dream, With Love, Passionate Life, Cyclamen, Orange Wallflower, Pussy Willow.

SUPPORTIVE MEASURES

Take a few moments every morning while washing to express appreciation and gratitude for all the gifts in our lives: – for the person who stopped to change the punctured tyre, for the hot water in the tap, the meal we ate last night, for the opportunities and freedom each day to connect, to learn, to make choices, to heal and to love, and for the beauty and wonder of the world about us.

Think about the words we use and remember that energy follows attention. Whatever we draw attention to will become energised. Avoid gossiping and complaining. Express appreciation to others. Share inspiration. Say no with love.

Listen to uplifting music, maybe join a choir. Try to sing out loud (even if only when alone in the shower, or in the car).

Cherry Plum Fruit

Prunus serasifera

"Pain is resistance to feeling"

Indications: fear of feeling; fear of powerful feelings; fear of breakdown, overwhelm or collapse; for catharsis and strong emotional release of anger, grief, fear etc.; for whenever we feel uncentered by strong feelings and become reactive or disconnected from feeling; for the heart, solar plexus, sacral and base chakras.

The message of Cherry Plum Fruit is that strong feelings and catharsis bring with them great gifts – the seeds of transformation, re-birth, and self-knowledge. Cherry Plum Fruit encourages us to stay peacefully in the heart of feeling, without reacting to, or suppressing what we feel out of fear or judgement. By staying still and centred, in the heart of feeling – in the eye of the storm, we come to know and understand ourselves better.

Cherry Plum Fruit shows us that there is nothing to fear in feeling. It is our resistance to feeling that creates our suffering. All that we uncover when we allow ourselves to feel – is greater love, self-knowledge and understanding, and we will always reach, beneath all our feelings, a well of infinite love, peace and understanding.

This applies whether these feelings are of anger, grief, fear, or even powerful joy. Underneath all the layers of feeling, underneath the tears and the rage, even beneath our terror and panic we will always uncover love and a deep experience of peace, because infinite peace and infinite love are our true nature. It is only our fear and judgement and our lack of understanding of ourselves that has caused us to bury our innocence and light – to separate ourselves from the experience of our innate peace and love.

All too often, when waves of strong emotion rise up and rush through us, we become afraid. We push these feelings away in fear, either splattering our emotions onto the world around us in violent reaction or panic, or burying them deep within us to become demons lurking in the cupboard, aspects of our experience that we are afraid to embrace.

Breakdown and instability occur when we react to a release of powerful feelings with fear and judgement and violent reaction. By peacefully embracing all that we feel, without judgement or reaction, we lose our fear of ourselves and of our feelings.

Cherry Plum Fruit is not only useful when catharsis occurs. Used on an ongoing basis, it encourages us to embrace, acknowledge and own our feelings as they arise, without judgement or fear, becoming conscious of how we feel throughout the day and aware of how these feelings affect our actions and choices. In this way we no longer suppress how we feel, or explode so often in reaction or panic when some event triggers the release of long held emotions. We learn to know and trust ourselves and our ability to embrace whatever arises in our experience, without losing our peace or our centre. We become detectives in our own lives searching for clues with which to understand ourselves better.

SUPPORTIVE MEASURES

It is important, if we are to become self-knowing, that we allow ourselves time to feel. Many of us have created lives that hardly leave us room to breathe, let alone to connect with how we are feeling. In the rush of keeping it all together, combined with our fear and judgement of what we might be feeling, emotions are pushed away until they build up and shout so loud that we can no longer ignore their insistent message that something needs to be dealt with.

Some of us are so adept at suppressing our feelings that we manage to bury how we feel for most of our lives, until our bodies or our hearts can no longer cope with being the repositories of so much unreleased tension and we find ourselves stopped in our tracks by emotional breakdown or illness.

If we take a few minutes alone every morning or evening to connect with ourselves, we can check in with how we are feeling and what we need to do in order to love and support ourselves. In this way we become self-knowing and are not so thrown by our emotions

By gently pulling on the threads of an underlying emotion we bring these feelings into our consciousness and we can begin to identify what it is that we are feeling and what it is that we are dealing with in our lives in that moment. Sometimes beneath slight irritations or anxieties lie deeper unresolved issues. As we allow ourselves to feel we begin to understand ourselves better.

When our emotions are running strong and we feel confused, it helps to write down all that we are feeling, without worrying about spelling or grammar – simply writing and writing until there is nothing more to say. This enables us to bring our feelings into the light of day so that we can see what it is that we are actually dealing with. Then we can look for the opportunity in this experience – for what it is showing us – what its gift is.

Often with emotional release comes tears and sobbing, which can be profoundly healing if surrendered to. Cherry Plum Fruit combined with Letting Go, Heart Flow and Blue Delphinium, can help release and allow the flow of long held tears. When we are full of rage and anger, some therapies advocate the use of emotional release activities – such as hitting a pile of cushions with a stick, or smashing old crockery against a wall, but these actions simply push our feelings outside ourselves and leave us exhausted, and disconnected from the heart of feeling. Instead we need to hold and keep safe the child inside us that feels afraid and grief stricken. This child inside wants to be loved, understood and held until the storm has passed. We need to remember that all anger arises out of our fearful perceptions – fear of being annihilated, fear of being rejected and alone – fear of love being withheld.

An important thing to understand is that however distraught we may be feeling, there is always a part of our essential self (you could call it our true parent self) – that is observing what is happening, and that is capable of taking responsibility for our actions and for keeping us safe. By connecting with this still point within we can check to see what it is that we need to do at any time in order to feel centred, safe and self-embracing.

In her transformational book "The Journey", Brandon Bays has put together two very simple, profound processes that anyone can follow, to uncover and heal the emotional root of any long-standing difficulty or illness in their lives. The two processes, called 'The Emotional Journey' and 'The Physical Journey' take no longer than two hours each to complete. It is now possible to buy tapes to guide one through the process or there are workshops and people throughout the UK and abroad, trained in this work, who guide people through these processes. (see Suggested Reading List and Useful Addresses).

See also: Blue Delphinium, Physostegia, Honesty, Phoenix Rebirth, Original Innocence, Inner Fire, Red Deadnettle, Red Quince, Heart Flow, Stitchwort, Cyclamen, Pink Cherry, Sweet Hunza, Sweet Pea.

Child's Play

Divine Child Essence (Inspirational Light Essence)

*"And he said ""Truly I say unto you, unless ye become as little children,
ye cannot enter the kingdom of heaven"" Matthew 18 v.2*

Indications: for whenever we have forgotten how to laugh and play, and
how to use our imagination; for over-seriousness, negativity, and a
limited, rigid, attitude towards life; for creative play and dreaming

❄

Child's Play is the essence of the innocent divine child, dancing and
playing, and spinning the world into being with ripples of laughter,
light and joy. It hands us the key to heaven and tells us that
awakening/enlightenment is Child's Play.

This essence reminds us that we are all divine, innocent, creative
beings with the ability to transform our world by our combined
thoughts and feelings. As we realise this we allow our vision of life and
our world to become filled with the unlimited potential of unrestrained
joy and light.

Child's Play reminds us that we live in a world of pure energy – that
energy follows thought and feeling. We literally dream our world into
being – what we choose to believe and dream we create. We can choose
whether we dream with certainty of miracles, innocence, peace and
abundance; or of suffering, guilt, war and lack – and as we dream, so the
universe will respond.

This essence can be used whenever we have forgotten how to play
and have become too serious and negative in our outlook. It teaches us

how to lighten our life with joy and laughter, and innocent fun and play, and it shows us how we may create heaven on earth. Child's Play helps us to loosen up and to allow some fun and play and joy into our lives. When we are too linear and literal or lacking in imagination in our way of being, Child's Play helps us to relax and to use our imagination and creativity to explore new ways of expanding and opening up our experience of life.

Child's Play helps us to connect to our inner child and to it's need for fun and imaginative play. We can take this essence whenever we want to play or to use our imagination – whether we are partying, playing with our children, or exploring, art, drama or creative writing. It helps us to play and to open our imagination to a world of infinite possibilities and wonderful creativity.

Over-seriousness and an inability to play often has its roots in childhood, particularly if we had to grow up too quickly and become responsible for ourselves, while still children. This may have been compounded by a feeling of responsibility and concern for those around us – our parents or our siblings. This is particularly the case if we lost one or both our parents when we were young, or where one or both parents were elderly, suffered from mental illness, alcoholism or drug addiction, or were frequently ill or vulnerable.

Any of these situations can create a heavy or unpredictable atmosphere to grow up in. In these situations, the child often takes on a more parental role, at least in terms of feeling responsible for a childlike or uncentered parent. If one of the parents has periods of 'high' energy and enthusiasm coupled with irresponsible behaviour, the child in reaction, may become cautious, self-monitoring and self-controlled in an effort not to reproduce the behaviour of their parent.

If this has been our experience, then we may not trust ourselves to let go our control, fearing that if we do so, we may become uncentered. We may find it very hard to be silly, exuberant or enthusiastic about life, always fearing that it might lead to irresponsible or shameful behaviour, or to our damaging ourselves or those around us. We may be somewhat 'po-faced'. Our energy may be 'dampening' to those around us, our body language may be stiff and controlled and we may feel very threatened and unsettled if others around us become wild or playful.

Child's Play inspires us to 'lighten up'. It gently encourages us to open up to joy and fun – teaching our inner child that it is safe and wonderful to play – particularly after years of seriousness or after a time of grief. It reminds us that life isn't meant to be grim – and that if we allow it, it can be wonderful, miraculous, joyful and funny.

I gave Child's Play, in combination with Reunion and Blue Delphinium, to a seven-year-old boy who didn't know how to play. He took this combination for nine months. Prior to taking these essences he only understood the world in literal and linear terms. He couldn't understand fantasy or imagination at all and was afraid of anything that was not literal. He would get very upset when companions in the playground played imaginary games, and would stand in front of them screaming "You're not a wizard! You're not a wizard!"

This child had barely smiled in the previous year and didn't understand humour at all. He was unwilling to draw except if he could trace or copy an image. Asked to draw something from his imagination he refused because he felt threatened by the endless possibility this presented him with. It was the same with creative writing. He also became very upset if there was any disruption to his established and secure routine.

Within a week or two of taking this combination of essences he began to laugh to himself, and gradually to join in, and later to instigate, fantasy games. He began to draw and write creatively, enjoying poetry writing and speaking. He developed a wonderful and playful sense of humour and became less and less disturbed by changes in routine or by new environments or activities.

See also: Living the Dream, Pussy Willow, Reunion, Cyclamen, Celandine, Golden Blessings, Passionate Life.

Comfrey

Symphytum aspermum

"Infinite patience brings immediate reward"

Raj

Indications: impatience; for when we feel limited or restricted by circumstance, fighting or resisting the situation we are in; for daydreaming, inattention, forgetfulness, or avoidance of being in the now; for impatience with the process of healing; for when we live in the future, unable or unwilling to experience meaning or good in the now; for when we feel unable to be still or to meditate; for when we repeatedly make the same mistakes, because we avoid connecting with what's happening in situations out of fear, or boredom, or because the situation highlights painful unresolved areas that we are unwilling to address.

❊

Comfrey teaches us the lesson of Dynamic Patience. It shows us that patience is not a static, empty waiting space that we have to endure until we arrive at some place where we want to be. Instead, we realise that the present moment that we are in is a dynamic place, allowing infinite possibilities of experience, and that we get to where we are going, by embracing all the potential of where we are now.

Magic occurs when we become curious to know and embrace whatever opportunity life is offering us in the present moment. Situations we may have been resisting, offer us a treasure trove of wisdom, joy, and tremendous unforeseen potential for development and expansion of awareness. Interestingly, immediately we embrace what is happening and stop fighting, things start to move, and what we embrace transforms.

Comfrey inspires a sense of timelessness and infinity, encouraging a more still and meditative approach to life. Through its inspiration we begin to understand how everything that we experience is interconnected and interlinked. From close-up we often only see a very small part of the picture of our life, in which events as they happen can appear random and disconnected, but when we look back over time, we can see that the events of our life unfold to form a constantly developing, interlinking, complex and beautiful multi-dimensional pattern. Comfrey helps us to appreciate the depth and richness of the present moment. It is very grounding and settling, inspiring us to grasp the opportunity of the situation we are in.

If we are dissatisfied and impatient with our life now and have big dreams for the future but are unwilling to go through all the necessary steps to get there, Comfrey combined with Red Poppy, Speedwell, Wild Cyclamen, Disciple of the Heart and Living the Dream, helps us to willingly embrace the steps that we need to take in order to get from where we are now to where we wish to be. It grounds us and helps us to settle into what we need to do, and to enjoy it and to really learn from the process. In this way, we are far more likely to succeed in our aims than if we are impatient and half-hearted about the process.

On a vibrational, energetic level, Comfrey creates a fluid matrix, an environment which encourages creativity and development, in which continuing connections and interconnections can be made, and information can be received and communicated.

Comfrey is a very vigorous, long-lived perennial plant. It has deep, black-skinned, branching roots, with white, gummy, mucilaginous, fibrous flesh. It has rough, hairy, hollow stems, 2-3 feet high, much branched, ending in spiral racemes of drooping blue, pink, purple or white flowers. Its large lower leaves are abundant and covered in rough hairs.

The most noticeable features of Comfrey are its ability to renew itself vigorously, when cut, to reproduce itself rapidly from a tiny fragment of root, its ability to draw up minerals and trace elements from the subsoil, and the abundant mucilage present in all parts of the plant. Horticulturally, Comfrey leaves are regularly cut for mulching, compost, and the making of liquid manure. Each plant can be cut down to the ground several times in the year, and will rapidly re-grow, ready to be cropped again.

See also: Lilac, Speedwell, Pussy Willow, Beauty in the Eye, Golden Blessings, Cherry Plum Fruit, Sky Blue Comfrey, Grandmothers Arms, Winter Jasmine, Living the Dream, Celandine, Passionate Life, Physostegia, Stitchwort, Sweet Hunza, The Rose, Reunion, Father Sun, One Being, At the Heart of Being.

Crab Apple Fruit

Malus pumila

Indications: for when we feel guilty or ashamed of having created disease or damage through some failing on our part; for when we believe that we have created physical or mental illness as a result of our repeated 'negative' emotional or behavioural patterns, or through not taking good enough care of ourselves; for guilt, hopelessness and feelings of failure in relation to health and our ability to heal; belief that we only heal if we become perfect and pure; for all chakras

Since we have come to understand the mind/body connection, and have become aware of our need to take responsibility for what we create in our experience, including our health, we have unfortunately often confused responsibility with guilt. The problem with guilt is that it keeps us fixed in self-judgment and we tend to then feel that we will only heal when we have become a totally good and pure person. So long as we fix ourselves in guilt we are unable to experience our innate wholeness.

Crab Apple Fruit encourages us to let go of self-punishment around illness and our 'physical' or mental health. This essence addresses our perceptions of our body and mind, and of physical and mental illness, particularly when we feel guilty of having created disease or damage through some failing on our part, and when we feel that we cannot undo what we believe we have created. It helps us to let go these feelings of guilt, and any beliefs that we might have created 'irreparable' damage. It inspires us to 'wipe the slate clean' – to return our perception of our body and ourselves to one of ever fresh, ever new innocence and crystal clear purity, washed clean of all trace of suffering, pain and trauma.

Crab Apple Fruit asks us to look again at our beliefs about 'cause' and 'effect' in relation to our health. It encourages us to move away from self-blame and guilt about having 'created' physical or emotional damage – to an experience of innate wholeness and perfection. It also addresses self-destructive patterns arising out of "What the hell – I've messed myself up so much – why bother anymore?" It shows us that nothing we do can affect our essential inner wholeness and purity – and it encourages us to release our body from the judgements that we hold against it and against ourselves. It is only our perception of ourselves that becomes clouded, because we feel we have failed to live up to some false image that we have held against ourselves.

Crab Apple Fruit inspires us to experience once again the light, beauty and perfection of our body and of ourselves, as though newborn. It reminds us that we are not 'physical' beings but are in fact fluid 'energy' beings. What we think is what we create. The energy of who we are is a constantly changing movement of consciousness that reflects back to us all our thoughts, beliefs and perceptions. As such it will reflect back to us our love of ourselves and our perception of our essential wholeness, purity, perfection and innocence.

See also: Divine Being, White Yarrow, Green Alexanders, Cyclamen, Heart Mother, Golden Blessings, Stitchwort, Pussy Willow, Sky Blue Comfrey, Original Innocence and Living The Dream.

Crimean Snowdrop

Galanthus plicatus

Indications: post-traumatic shock and memories of suffering that haunt; for healing the memory of trauma and suffering wherever it is held in our being, in an environment or in material objects; for all chakras.

Crimean Snowdrop addresses how we perceive our memories of traumatic events. It encourages us to view these memories from the perspective of the Higher Self, rather than from the memory of our emotional reaction at the time. Often the trauma that we feel comes from the memory of our original emotional reaction and judgement at the time of an event, or from the memory of the emotional reactions and judgements of others involved.

One way in which we can heal these memories is to be able to see them as they actually were, rather than through the lens of judgement or fear. We can do this by returning to our memory of an event; allowing ourselves to settle into the feeling of that experience, and to remain in the midst of that feeling without reacting to it, and without trying to jump out of the experience. If we let go our judgement and fear and stay peacefully in the midst of feeling, breathing gently into that feeling and expanding it, with curiosity to see what it really feels like, we no longer feel powerless and we begin to be able to respond peacefully to what is happening.

By doing so we gain insight into how we may deal peacefully with any event in our lives – and respond appropriately, instead of running scared into powerless reactions of panic and shock. The trauma of our memories arises from the memory of leaving our inner sense of safety and security – of jumping out of our peace – in an attempt to escape from a situation.

Crimean Snowdrop shows us that our memory of an event is often the memory of our emotional reaction, or the emotional reaction of others at the time, rather than a memory of the true reality of that event. Crimean Snowdrop does not remove our memory of an event. Its healing lies in returning us to pure essence, to the true reality of an event, in divine terms, unclouded by fear, shock or judgement. It encourages us to experience an event from a divine perspective, from the viewpoint of our Higher Self, from our centre of peace and understanding.

This essence can be used to heal the memory of trauma and suffering that has been held within an environment or within material objects. It is a key essence in the space clearing combination "Lighter Space". Crimean Snowdrop on its own, or in combination with Original Innocence, can be added to a mister for clearing the energy of the home, and in accident and emergency rooms; drops may be added to water used for floor, surface and clothes washing. Bottles can be buried in the ground at accident sites and battlefields (combine with Phoenix Rebirth and Original Innocence for this purpose) and bottles may also be dropped into ponds, lakes or rivers that need clearing (combine with Phoenix Rebirth, Original Innocence and Living the Dream, for water clearing).

See also: Stitchwort, Cherry Plum Fruit, Original Innocence, Phoenix Rebirth, Letting Go, Red Clover, Crab Apple Fruit.

Cyclamen

Cyclamen sp. and Rose Quartz

Indications: exhaustion, burn out; no time and space for ourselves; not looking after ourselves; not following our dreams; no time to be creative; for anger and resentment; for when we allow our life to be governed by external demands; for when we give too much to others and don't look after our own needs; for loss of sense of self and loss of creativity and inspiration; for the heart, solar plexus and base chakras.

Many of us live lives in which we do not have enough time and space for ourselves. We allow our lives to be driven by external dictates, trying to fulfil roles and expectations, often disregarding our core inner needs and creative potential. Exhaustion, burn out, deep levels of stress, lack of fulfilment and a lack of sense of self, are all the results of living without connecting to our feelings, to our hearts, to our needs, and to our deep well of creativity.

We need to ask ourselves: "Do I have room to breathe and peace in my heart? Do I have time to connect with myself and with my own understanding? Is there space for me in my life or am I crowded out of the picture? Do I have time to rest and restore my energy and look after my body and play; do I allow myself the time to connect with how I am feeling? What governs my choices – love or fear? Who makes the choices in my life? What kind of life am I creating?"

Cyclamen is about living life from our heart, from a point of love and care for ourselves – creating lives which are rich and full, with time to nourish and care for ourselves, and time to nurture our body's need for rest, good food and exercise, and our soul's need for interest, inspiration, fun, peace, companionship, colour, and creative expression. Cyclamen inspires us to take time to look after ourselves properly, to develop our creativity and to manifest our dreams, knowing that whatever is loving and nurturing for us personally, will also benefit those around us.

When we find ourselves feeling repeatedly angry and resentful, this is generally because we are not taking the time and space that we need for ourselves – time to rest – time to play – time to be kind to ourselves and time to do the things that we love doing. Cyclamen is about having a life now, and being kind to ourselves now, not waiting until some time in the future when things may have eased or for when we retire. If we put our life and happiness on hold until some time in the future, by the time we reach that point (if ever) we may be too sick from accumulated stress and exhaustion to be able to enjoy a rich and full life.

Sometimes allowing ourselves the time to rest and enjoy life causes others around us to look at whether their lives are fulfilling or not. If they have chosen a hard way of being, they may feel resentful and jealous if they think that we are having an easier life than them. Cyclamen helps us to love and honour ourselves without giving in to outside pressure and judgement. In the west we make a virtue out of work and achievement and we pay a high price in terms of our health, our happiness, and our relationships. This is not to say that being busy or realising dreams is bad for us – however, Cyclamen inspires us to look at what kind of life we are creating and encourages us, on a daily basis, to find a more loving way to live our lives and to achieve our goals.

One of the reasons we don't allow ourselves the time and space that we need, is our fear of not having enough money unless we follow a certain (and often hard) way of 'earning' our abundance. For this reason it's often helpful to combine Cyclamen with the inspiration of Living the Dream, With Love, Disciple of the Heart, Pussy Willow and Heart Mother, in order that we can begin to know and trust that life will support us if we support and honour ourselves on a daily basis.

Doctrine of Signatures: This particular essence was made from a miniature cyclamen plant which lived in my office/den/sanctuary. It flowered almost continually for three years. As cyclamens grow from young plants into adult plants, they gradually develop a broad, heart shaped corm that contains a store of nourishment and moisture that they can draw on, and which sustains them through lean, dry periods.

In the wild cyclamens grow in the shade of trees in poor, dry soil, with few nutrients, surviving for many years because of their ability to create this corm. Their leaves are heart-shaped, the faces of the flowers look down as if in quiet consideration. The flowers of this pink cyclamen have an elusive, sweet perfume that is often only apparent when one gets close to them.

See also: Living the Dream, Pussy Willow, Grandmothers Arms, Heart Mother, Bluebell Grove, With Love, Speedwell, Disciple of the Heart, Cherry Plum Fruit, Goldenrod, Pink Cherry, Red Poppy, Blue Delphinium, Physostegia and Inner Fire.

SUPPORTIVE MEASURES

The druids have a word for the space that we inhabit which represents our individuality. The word is 'nemeton'. It describes the inner sanctuary of our being, the sacred grove of our hearts, the sacred circle in which we centre and connect with ourselves to find peace and understanding.

It can also be used to describe any place or sanctuary in which we can connect with our inner space. This may be a quiet space in our home, or somewhere in the landscape where we feel at home.

Obviously, our home is within our heart and it is here that true peace is found. However, most of us find it hard to stay centred within the stillness of our heart space, amidst the hustle and bustle of daily life.

One of the first steps we can take in nurturing ourselves is to create time and space for ourselves. If we are carers, we need to arrange to have regular time off. All of us need a time during the day where we can centre and connect with ourselves and with how we are feeling. We also need time to relax, recharge and re-inspire ourselves.

Having undisturbed time on our own, every day can make a real difference to our life and to how we feel about ourselves. In our 'time out' we can rest, relax, connect with our feelings and guidance, meditate, read, dream, reflect, study, write, paint, develop ideas etc. This helps us to restore our energy, to become more self-knowing and to develop a greater individual sense of self.

We also benefit greatly from having a small area of physical space on this planet that is ours alone. By creating a personal sanctuary in our life we create a focal point for connecting with ourselves and with our heart – a place that reflects who we are, and our individual interests, dreams, creativity, inspiration, and intention.

Ideally this space would be a room of one's own. In my ideal world everyone would have a room of their own, which they could decorate, furnish and fill with whatever was meaningful, inspiring and personal to them. Since for many this is not possible, we might claim a corner of a room, where we could place a table or desk, some shelves and a comfy chair – and some personal objects that reflect who we are back to us. We might keep our favourite books there, inspiring pictures, plants, paints, stones, a candle etc. In this way we can make an altar to our life – a place to focus and connect with ourselves and with our heart. Owning a personal space represents owning our lives – inhabiting and being the authors of our lives – creating a life that reflects back to us who we essentially are.

Disciple of the Heart

Willow – Salix viminalis

Indications: for when we react to or avoid, any form of discipline, organisational structure or standards – either by rebelling, or by resorting to displacement or mind-numbing activities; for when we feel a failure because we have not found it possible to live and work according to certain material, organisational or spiritual standards or ideals; for those who wish to create heart-impelled creative ways of working and living, and fluid, responsive structures; for the heart, brow, solar plexus and base chakras.

Disciple of the Heart inspires us to understand the nature of true discipline, which arises from our hearts as an internal, fluid, flexible response to the reality of life as it actually is. It shows us a new way of being – a bubbling flow of creative loving being – trusting in our own innate goodness and perfection.

Disciple of the Heart encourages us to find our own heart-impelled ways to organise our lives, so that we can follow our dreams and manifest them in the world. It encourages us to be kinder and more understanding of our child/self – to embrace our need for play and for life to be more creative and loving – and not so adult and serious. Whenever we feel inadequate because we feel we are unable to live up to some standard or ideal, Disciple of the Heart inspires us to love and to trust ourselves, and our own innate goodness.

Disciple of the Heart also inspires those who are trying to create more fluid, responsive, organisational structures, and more humane ways of working within businesses and organisations.

Sometimes our false beliefs around discipline and structure derive from past lives in religious orders, or from childhood and teenage experiences, growing up in environments steeped in strong religious or cultural ideals and standards, and prejudicial judgements of 'right' or 'wrong' ways of being, or doing things.

When we impose an ideal or standard on ourselves, rather than living from our hearts, we become internally conflicted between head (ideals and standards) and heart (truth). We may hide this well as we try to conform to whatever image of perfection we are trying to live up to, but inside our child is desperately crying because the joy of living has gone from our lives.

When we impose discipline, inflexible structure and spiritual ideals on ourselves we do not recognise our own innate goodness and perfection – we do not trust that we can achieve things without constant attempts to discipline and order our unruly child self. We may seek relief from our disciplined lifestyle in drink, drugs, food, t.v. and other mind numbing pursuits, or we may reach crisis or breakdown when the child within us finally rebels at having been suppressed and ignored for so long.

If we have children, the way that we suppress our own inner child is often mirrored in the way that we as parents treat our children, and in how our children react when discipline or structure is imposed upon them.

Some of us react to old material and spiritual standards and structures, by rejecting or rebelling against any situation that might involve structure, morality, discipline or self-discipline. As a result, we avoid stretching ourselves, or developing our talents, and consequently, at some level, we feel deeply unfulfilled. This lack of fulfilment and lack of confidence in our own abilities is often buried in a hedonistic lifestyle, with daytimes spent working in a job that is undemanding and un-stretching – and evenings or time off spent in pursuit of whatever will numb or displace our deep lack of self worth – we may drink heavily, take drugs, over-eat, watch television and videos for hours, play computer games or use sex as a drug.

Cut off from ourselves and from a real connection to life – avoiding situations or opportunities that might demand some form of self discipline, self organisation or a degree of commitment, we do not give the gift of who we are to the world and we do not fulfil our true potential – it is as though we are stuck in rebellious teenage reaction that lasts long after teenage years have passed.

Many of us have this dynamic to a greater or lesser degree, particularly when we are trying to avoid something that requires structured work, or that might stretch us in some way. We fill time with displacement activities, take repeated cigarette breaks, eat endless snacks, browse catalogues, mindlessly surf the internet, hoover the house repeatedly, read last weeks paper – anything to avoid getting down to that piece of coursework, filling in our tax return forms, or writing that book!

Disciple of the Heart encourages us to expand our vision of how we might accomplish things, so that we no longer react against structure, but instead find our own unique way of structuring our life and work – a way that comes from our heart, that is flexible and personal to each of us and to our individual circumstances.

See also: Living the Dream, With Love, Lilac, Pussy Willow, Red Poppy, Passionate Life, Cyclamen, Heart Mother and The Rose.

Divine Being

Achillea millefolium and clear quartz

Indications: feeling powerless, vulnerable or dis-empowered; fear of illness; for whenever we feel vulnerable to environmental pollution, radiation, viruses, cancer; for when we feel vulnerable to other people's emotional and psychic energy, or to psychic or physical attack etc; for lack of confidence in our ability to heal ourselves; for fear of standing fully in our light and power.

Divine Being addresses our perceptions about vulnerability and about whether we need to protect or defend ourselves from 'outside attack' or 'harmful' outside influences. It reminds us that we are not mere mortals – but are instead divine energy beings creating our reality through what we think and what we feel. It reminds us that there is no such thing as 'physical' matter. What we think and what we believe is what we create. As divine beings, our world mirrors back to us our conscious and sub-conscious beliefs, perceptions and fears.

What we resist persists – what we embrace transforms. When we resist something we draw back from that experience in self-defence. Divine Being encourages us to expand our light into all areas of our experience – to no longer withdraw in fear from an experience, instead to breathe gently and peacefully into our resistance, to fill the whole of our experience with our peace. The more we embrace our fears with love and with divine awareness, the more we realise just how powerful we are. This is not power over others, rather it is the power of our divine peace and the recognition of the divine in all things and all beings.

Divine Being encourages us to embrace our frightened inner child and our limited mortal sense of self, with the peace of divine awareness. The more we recognise the divine nature of our being and of life, the more we will find the divine reflected back to us in our experience.

When we lack confidence in our ability to heal, this essence reminds us that our body is not a 'physical' body but an energy body, and that energy follows thought. In this way, our body reflects back to us our thoughts, beliefs, perceptions and feelings about ourselves and about our world. Divine Being encourages us to expand the light and peace of our divine self, into every atom, cell and fibre of our whole being. As we embrace ourselves and life with divine awareness, 'miracles' occur and we may soon begin to realise that 'miracles' are an everyday fact of divine being!

When we relax and expand into a situation that we feel threatened by, we create a shift in energy – from fear into safety and peace. This shift communicates itself, to our body, to those people around us and to the world in general. Cranio-sacral therapist Paul Parolin once said to me "When your heart is defended – energetically it's like waving a red flag to a bull, saying, "Come and get me!"" When we expect attack, we attract attack. If on some level we do not trust ourselves, others also will mistrust us.

Divine Being reminds us that there is no such thing as evil – simply an absence of the recognition of love, and the divine. It helps us to become aware of the mirrors in our life that reflect back to us our own beliefs and perceptions about ourselves, and about life. It encourages us to gradually let go of trying to defend or protect ourselves against things that we feel might harm us. It shows us that our fear of harm is no security at all – and that by withdrawing divine awareness from an area of our experience, we reinforce the perception that we are vulnerable and powerless, and we draw to us that which we fear. It is as though we leave a void to be filled by that which we fear.

Divine Being reminds us that we are immortal and invulnerable – that nothing can harm our essential being. The re-awakening of our Divine Self is a conscious process. As we become more aware of our thoughts and beliefs, and our choices based on those thoughts and beliefs, we begin to realise how truly divine we are – how we shape our world, and how we have the choice to create heaven on earth at this time.

Divine Being resonates with the teaching of the Chenresig/Avalokitesvara mantra 'Om Mani Padme Hum', and the light, love, liberation, and freedom from suffering, embodied within that mantra.

See also: Stitchwort, True Power, Red Clover, Peaceful Detachment, Living the Dream, Sky Blue Comfrey, Crimean Snowdrop, Crab Apple Fruit, Heart Flow, Loving Me – Loving You, At the Heart of Being, Original Innocence, Inner Fire, Red Poppy, Speedwell, Violet, The Rose.

Father Sun

Inner Heart Essence – Sonchus arvensis

Indications: for feelings of vulnerability, lack of strength and fear of being unable to cope on one's own in the world without strong support; for lack of confidence in independently managing one's financial and legal affairs; for grief or anticipatory grief over the loss of one's father or male partner or friend; for when we long for a strong, caring,supportive, male partner, or presence in our lives; for children who do not have a strong, caring male role model in their lives; for late summer and autumnal grief at losing the warmth and light of the sun with the approach of winter.

❋

Father Sun helps us to embody the archetype of the divine Father Sun within our own heart and being, It reminds us that we have within us a radiant positive divine Father Self, in whose unconditionally loving arms we can enfold our inner child whenever it feels vulnerable and in need of strength, support and guidance.

Father Sun shows us how to comfort, support and counsel ourselves – to realise that we have within us the strength, support, guidance and positivity that we have sought from others. By re-connecting with our own divine Sun Father/Self we are able to comfort and reassure our inner child, banishing its fears with the positive, revitalising warmth and light of the sun – and restoring courage, strength, purpose and the confidence to independently manage our worldly affairs and interact successfully in the outside world.

Father Sun helps to heal old grief and the feelings of vulnerability, lack of strength and longing for support, that often arise in reaction to the loss of one's father, the loss of a male partner or the loss of a supportive male friend. Sometimes this essence is called for prior to the event of losing our father or male partner, for grief in anticipation of the loss of their support and physical presence.

This essence also relates to sons and daughters leaving home, who need to learn how to support themselves as they move out into the world. In archetypal terms the father is the positive male role model who shows us how to embody the inner strength, centredness and courage that we need in order to go out into the world, and manage our worldly affairs independently, and deal with the hustle and bustle of life.

Father Sun is often indicated for children from single parent families where the mother is the sole carer, or in families where the father is unable to provide a strong, caring, male role model, confident in managing his affairs in the world. Learning how to embody these qualities is important both for boys and for girls but especially so for boys.

Boys have a real need for inspiring, caring male role models, particularly from the age of seven right through their continuing growth and development into manhood. They need someone who will, motivate and praise them, who will recognize their qualities and potential, support their development, help them to understand themselves and others, and encourage them to value their own integrity and respect the integrity of others.

If we have had someone around us during our formative years, who was confident in their dealings with the world, then it is much easier for us to feel confident and positive about getting out into the world as we become adults. If however, those around us in our childhood were not able to function adequately and confidently in the world, or if our father was not present because of relationship break-up or death, then it can be a lot harder for us when the time comes for us to go out into the world.

Women who lose their fathers when children, or who have had fathers, or mothers and fathers, who did not cope well in the world, often find it hard to 'get out there' and may seek a strong male father figure, or a confident woman, as a partner, to protect them and to help them to deal with the world. Men, who grow up without a positive male role model, particularly if their father is dysfunctional, may go through a very confused emotional period in their teenage years and early twenties, where they struggle with not having a strong inner sense of who they are and what their purpose might be. Often they find it hard to develop their talents and gifts in a way that they can manifest and integrate into the world. Because of lack of confidence, lack of clear sense of purpose and lack of fulfillment, they may drift into drink and drug taking and as a consequence end up in trouble with authority.

Father Sun also helps those who are sensitive and have a strong connection to moon, water and earth energy, but perhaps lack a great deal of fire energy: Father Sun helps us to embody within us the lion-hearted, masculine radiance of the sun in order that we may feel robust and confident enough to fully interact with the world.

This essence also addresses our anxiety and grief over losing the warmth and light of the sun as autumn begins. It inspires us to find ways to warm and strengthen our body and spirit through the cold, dark days of winter – to keep the sun shining in our hearts throughout the year.

See also: Goldenrod, Inner Fire, Red Poppy, Passionate Life, Physostegia, Blue Delphinium, Living the Dream, Disciple of the Heart, Comfrey and Heart Mother.

Grandmother's Arms

Inner Heart Essence – Hawthorn Blossom

Indications: for whenever we put ourselves or others under pressure to go faster and do more, and neglect to listen to our own needs or to the needs of others; for whenever we are internally conflicted between the needs and desires of our busy adult/self, and our child/self; for whenever we have lost touch with an holistic way of being and with what is healing for all; for when we wish to make a deeper connection to the healing that is found in Nature; for the heart, solar plexus and base chakras.

This essence helps us to embody the archetype of the Grandmother/Wise Woman/Ancient Mother within our own heart and being. It reminds us that we can connect within ourselves to our own deep wisdom and timeless knowledge of healing, as embodied and passed down by the Grandmother and by the wise women throughout the ages in many cultures.

Grandmothers Arms is often particularly useful for those who were abandoned, rejected, neglected or abused by their mothers. For these people even the word 'mother' can seem a dirty word, and they can become quite upset at the idea of working with essences to do with the mother, or with mothering, because they have such painful memories from their relationship with their own mother. Grandmothers Arms offers a less threatening, and less painful way to connect to an unconditional mother energy, and it can provide a way to begin to heal the wounds of the inner child.

The Grandmother comforts and protects the child, and champions its cause. Reconnecting with the spiritual archetype of the Grandmother and embodying that love and wisdom within our own being ensures that we always listen to the child in our heart – that its voice is always heard, its needs are met and its growth and development of wisdom and knowledge is always nurtured. The Grandmother removes potential conflict from our hearts by ensuring that all the aspects of our inner being remain in dialogue together and work together for the benefit of all.

The Grandmother maintains a comfortable pace, never hurrying, always ensuring that the child in her heart is free from pressure, even when there is a need to move quickly. She knows deeply the true nature of time – the true timing of things – the rhythms, seasons and cycles of life. She is master of balance on all levels. By embodying this knowing within our hearts we walk in peace, at a comfortable pace, that heals and brings stability and joy to our life.

The Grandmother holds within her the knowledge of healing on all levels. Through her embodiment we rediscover our own intuitive knowledge of what will heal our body, heart and soul. We revive our own deep connection to the healing spirit in all Nature, and our innate knowledge of the healing spirit of the plants, trees, animals, birds, rivers, fish, seas, elements, sun, moon and stars.

Carrying within her all the wisdom and understanding of babe, girl, maid, woman, mother and grandmother, the Grandmother knows how to heal all the wounds of the heart. In embodying this healing within ourselves, we hold our heart child safe within the embrace of strong, gentle wise arms, and with immeasurable love, encouragement and wisdom, restore wholeness, strength, joy and laughter.

See also: Heart Mother, Rosebay Willowherb, Pussy Willow, Cyclamen, Speedwell, Wild Cyclamen and Pink Cherry.

Green Alexanders

Smyrnium olustratum

Indications: lack of confidence in our physicality and robustness, low energy and vitality, reluctance to take physical exercise, disconnection from the natural world and the elements; feeling uncomfortable with the changing weather, seasons and temperatures.

❄

Green Alexanders helps us to enjoy being physically alive and vital. It heightens our awareness of the 'chi' life force energy of this world, inspiring us to connect to this re-vitalising energy and light – to breathe it into every cell of our being, to raise our own 'chi' energy and life force. The greatest source of this life force energy is found outside in fresh air and among plants and trees, and in nature.

Many of us spend the greater part of each day indoors, in artificial lighting, leading a largely sedentary lifestyle surrounded by electromagnetic technology. Inevitably our vitality is lowered by this way of life, and we become sluggish and lacking in zest for life. Green Alexanders re-connects us to the natural world, to our body, to the joy of being physically alive and active, and to breathing in fresh air and feeling uplifted and renewed by being out in the natural world, the elements and the changing weather and seasons.

Green Alexanders is an extraordinary plant. It remains green throughout most of the year. In the harshest of winters its leaves grow green and lush – even in January when almost all other soft green herbaceous plants have withered and turned brown in the frost, this plant looks as fresh as any leafy young plant would in springtime. It can also grow in the hottest, driest places without losing its vigour and lushness. It is as though it contains its own anti-freeze and its own wellspring of vitality, and as though it's very green-ness and vitality wakes us up to how we can re-build our own vitality and life-force.

As we work with this essence we may begin to become aware of the light and energy of the life force in the air all around us when we are outside – or we may find that we can breathe in chi energy and green-ness from the plants that we pass. We may find ourselves uplifted and re-energised by the wind, or by being out in the rain – we may feel blessed by the sun, or exhilarated by a storm or by the waves crashing on a beach.

Green Alexanders helps us to really begin to notice this life force around us, and the ways in which we can draw on this vibrant energy to renew our own 'chi' vitality. Being outside, away from electro-magnetic sources and surrounded by negative ions also helps to balance and clear the effects of too many hours spent around computers, televisions and microwaves – all of which deplete our vital force.

Drawing on the inspiration of this essence we may once again begin to feel the natural joy of our youth – the joy of moving our body, the excitement of remembering what it feels like to walk, run, cycle, swim or dance, and to feel our energy beginning to move again. Green Alexanders encourages us to begin to move and breathe again – to come alive – to breathe life into ourselves – to re-build our physical vitality and stamina through exercise, and to rediscover the joy of being alive and active in a body, out in this beautiful world.

If we are sensitive to changes in temperature and the weather, this essence helps us to feel more relaxed and more able to embrace all weathers and all temperatures – to love the changing seasons, and to welcome their differing energies.

See also: Passionate Life, Stitchwort, Divine Being, Red Clover, Sky Blue Comfrey, Cyclamen, Grandmothers Arms, Rosebay Willowherb, One Being, Bluebell Grove, Golden Blessings, Crab Apple Fruit, Winter Jasmine, Father Sun.

Golden Blessings

Golden autumn leaves of Acer platanoides

Indications: discontented; never fully satisfied; always hungry for more or for something different; waiting for things to get better; unappreciative; feeling empty; restless; critical; self-critical; fear of lack; unable to give; unhappy with 'imperfection' or with one's own 'imperfection.'

Gratitude, feeling blessed, appreciation; contentment; feeling abundant; creating joy, happiness and golden moments – no matter what is happening nor where we are in the cycle of life; happy with change and imperfection; happy to be in the now; letting go of the past and the future; not needing things, or ourselves to be 'perfect, in order to appreciate and enjoy life; sharing our blessings and our gifts and talents with others – not hanging on to things.

Golden Blessings and Heart Mother both address a feeling of emptiness, of always lacking something – of never enough – a hunger that is never satisfied by material possessions, food, drink, sex, or smoking. These things can temporarily numb a feeling of emptiness, but they do not fill the void inside us. This is because we look in the wrong place for satisfaction – always reaching forward to the next thing, never fully savouring where we are and what we have. We will find satisfaction when we slow down and allow ourselves to experience the gift and nourishment of what we have, in the moment that we are in.

Golden Blessings encourages us to enjoy and make the most of every moment, every mouthful, every sip – to appreciate every thing that we have – both in material terms, as well as in terms of all the qualities and gifts in our lives. It helps us to deeply appreciate our friends, our relationships (even when difficult), our family, people in our lives who have helped us, opportunities for growth, our work, the challenges in our lives, our talents and abilities, the place we are, the flowers in the park, the clothes we have, the food on our tables, our home, hot water, heating, our pets etc. There is so much to be grateful for and to enjoy and Golden Blessings shows us that we are constantly blessed with everything that we need, just when we need it.

If we are always waiting for things to get better, then we never experience where we are now. We never see who we are with, the gift that they bring – and the gift that we can give. If we find giving difficult because we don't feel that we have enough, Golden Blessings can inspire us to fully receive and appreciate the gifts that we have. Once we feel truly gifted, then we may feel abundant enough to be happy to give, This isn't about giving with no boundaries, but it is about when we do decide to give, really giving, without any hidden agendas about what we might expect in return.

This essence shows us that we can have all the riches in the world and still not feel satisfied. There is nothing wrong in having beautiful things and wonderful gifts, but we live in a world of change and we need to be able to let go continually, and we need to appreciate where we are and what we have in any moment. We can lose anything or anyone at any time, and that loss is far worse if we have not appreciated what we've had, when we've had it.

Our joy, our love, and the love and appreciation that we bring to whatever situation we are in, however grim or 'imperfect', creates a golden experience for us and for others – one that all the money in the world can't buy. This is unconditional love – the love that recognises that which is real in each and every thing – that blesses each moment, each morsel of food and each person it encounters, and that recognises in love, the Divine in all beings and all things. This is what truly satisfies, sustains and nourishes.

See also: Celandine, Beauty in the Eye, Comfrey, Crab Apple Fruit, Loving Me – Loving You, Orange Wallflower, Speedwell, With Love, Pussy Willow, Sweet Hunza, Grandmothers Arms, Heart Mother.

Goldenrod

Solidago virgaurea

Indications: for when we feel diminished, crushed or humiliated by another's criticism or judgement; for when we neglect to honour our integrity and our inner knowing; for when we submit to external dictates, authority figures, peer group or societal pressure, or to an image we try to live up to; for rebelliousness and resentment.

For when we attract bullying or patronising behaviour as well as for when we bully others; for those who find it hard to be on their own; for low self esteem, self doubt and lack of confidence in expressing our own individual point of view or understanding; for when we are afraid to disagree with those who are more confident in their opinions; for when we lack confidence in our own understanding and wisdom, and are needy of approval, respect and recognition from others.

Goldenrod encourages us to value our own individual understanding – not from a need to be right, but from a recognition of our own individual right to express an opinion, and to question the authority or verity of information or opinions given or held by others. Its energy is grounding and centering, encouraging us to be self-responsible and self-referring – to honour and trust our own inner knowing and to peacefully assert and honour our own integrity and inner authority. It empowers us to feel able to stand our ground, to say no, and to be confident enough to set appropriate boundaries in our relationships.

Difficulties with lack of self-respect, and issues with authority often arise from our childhood relationship with our father, and are influenced by the type of role model our father presented to us – whether he was present at all during our childhood; whether he knew how to peacefully assert himself; whether he was lacking in confidence or had difficulties with authority and structure in his life, whether he was a weak parent, or whether he was domineering or aggressive towards us. (If our father was not present during our childhood and teenage years, our role models may have come from other men, or from strong women around us who demonstrated positive or negative masculine qualities).

If our father was able to honour his own integrity, to listen to his own counsel, to peacefully assert and express himself, and to deal with authority and structure in his life – then we may have grown up learning how to embody these abilities in our own life. However, when our father was either absent, weak or over domineering, and we did not have supportive, confident and peacefully assertive role models in other adults (whether male or female), who were close to us in our childhood, then we may well lack confidence now in honouring our integrity and in dealing positively with authority and structure.

Depending on our personality, and whether we are fiery, or not, we will react differently to this lack of a peacefully assertive role model. If we have little fire in our make-up, then we may respond to authority, domineering behaviour or structure, by feeling crushed, frozen, timid, and unable to speak out. We may feel unable to honour ourselves, and our individual right to express an opinion, or to question another's authority. From a very young age we may lack self-respect and may be afraid to stand our ground. We may repeatedly attract bullying or patronising behaviour, and feel powerless and intimidated by those in authority or by authoritarian structure. We may also be stuck in childlike behaviour, trying to control our relationships, by pleasing others in order to gain favour, or by playing the role of victim, in order to gain sympathy or attention.

If we are more fiery by nature, we may react to this lack of positive parenting, by showing off and by bullying others in order to hide our lack of self-worth. We may be rebellious and confrontational with authority, and defensively aggressive towards others. This type of behaviour, although less passive, nonetheless springs from an essential lack of self-respect and genuine confidence, since rebelliousness is a reaction to external authority instead of a peaceful assertion of one's own authority.

Goldenrod teaches us to respect ourselves and to respect others – to value our own equal right to be, and to express ourselves, and the right of others to be, and to express themselves. It encourages us to peacefully and assertively take charge of our lives, to listen to, and honour, our own inner wisdom and counsel, and to be happy to think and act as an individual.

This is an essence for individuation, and peaceful self-assertion. It often relates to teenagers who are struggling to find their own identity, in relation to authority and in relation to peer group pressure and influence. It also addresses those times when we know that we need to leave a relationship, or a group that we are a part of, and are afraid to do so because we do not feel strong or confident enough to stand alone. It gives us the courage to walk our own path, to support ourselves and to begin to enjoy our own company and counsel, and it encourages us to build new relationships, from a standpoint of greater self-respect and integrity.

Whenever we have a need to grasp our power and to become empowered as an individual in our own right, Goldenrod encourage us to listen peacefully to our own inner voice, and to respond to our inner knowing, regardless of who might tell us that we are wrong, or that they have greater authority or understanding than we do. It encourages us to seek within for the counsel, approval, support and recognition that we have sought from others.

See also: Blue Delphinium, Physostegia, Red Poppy, Loving Me – Loving You, Father Sun, Inner Fire, Blue Salvia, Honesty, Red Quince, True Power, Violet, Disciple of the Heart, The Rose, Yellow Hyacinth, At the Heart of Being, Pure Love.

Heart Flow

Amaryllis belladonna (crimson)

Indications: for those who feel that they have an emotional weight or an emotional tight fist pressing on their heart; for whenever we carry painful memories in our hearts which cause us to react defensively; for when we take things personally, or defend our hearts out of fear of pain and suffering. For opening the heart chakra (front and back).

❄

Heart Flow shows us that when we defend our heart as a reaction against possible judgement, rejection or fear, we do not experience safety. We are always watching our back afraid of encountering experiences which will trigger painful memories locked in our heart.

Heart Flow encourages us to open our heart to love – to embrace and let go the memory of old pain and suffering and defence. Our suffering lies in our clinging to an individual identity. Freedom from suffering arises when we become simply the movement of consciousness, embracing and responding to life moment by moment – inhaling and exhaling – embracing and letting go.

We take things personally when we think that we are fixed individual beings who may be hurt. It is our fear of feeling and our resistance to feeling that causes us to defend our hearts, and to restrict the flow of love through our heart. This ever-present love is our life-blood and birth right.

Those feelings we have been afraid to feel remain buried in our hearts. Their memories haunt us whenever we encounter experiences with similar resonance. Heart Flow encourages us to embrace these feelings, with love and understanding, to let them go and to move on with a free heart. It shows us how we may keep our heart open and responsive, so that the energy of love can flow freely and continually through it, unimpeded.

Heart Flow inspires us to let go of identifying ourselves as a fixed personality – to experience instead simply being the movement of love – responding moment by moment to life – allowing feelings to flow through our heart rather than defending ours heart and restricting or shutting down the flow of living Love.

This essence helps us at this time, as we begin to awaken and integrate true divine nature within our awareness here in this lifetime. Our true nature is not confined by identity or a fixed personality, but rather is boundless and fluid. Our heart holds the key to awakening through our willingness to embrace and to let go of old pain, fear, defence, and the limitation of identity.

See also – Cherry Plum Fruit, Red Quince, Pure Love, Red Deadnettle, Phoenix Rebirth, Honesty, Blue Delphinium.

Heart Mother

Cyclamen and clear quartz

Indications: for when we have experienced inadequate or excessive mothering; for when we either over cosset ourselves and are unadventurous and over needy of security, or push ourselves too hard and deny ourselves nurture or emotional support; for when we over cosset and dis-empower our children, or are too hard on them and not sufficiently nurturing and supportive of their needs; for when we give too much to others.

For all who are carers (whether male or female) who need to 'get a life' for themselves outside of caring; for when we are always trying to 'help' others in order to create an identity of 'worth' for ourselves; for mood swings – extremes of highs and lows, and swings between neediness and self-denial; for difficulty managing our resources – in terms of energy or finances; for when cannot control our hunger for love, food, sex or material goods; for when we feel so deprived that we take without respect and without giving in return; for the heart, solar plexus and base chakras.

❄

This essence is for embodying the archetypal mother within us – the strong, gentle, wise, beautiful mother who empowers and gives enough but does not smother. She carries within her the child, who she nurtures enough but who she also encourages to leave the safety of her arms in order that it may explore life and grow through the wisdom of experience.

Heart Mother respects her own need to be an adult and also to have time to rest and play and create. She does not allow herself to be eaten up by the needs of her child, nor does she find her identity solely in her role as a mother or nourisher – she is a beautiful creative being in her own right, with her own destiny and path. She knows she neither owns the child, nor does the child own her. She is Mother Earth and embodies, abundance, nurture, creativity, darkness and light, and seasons and life cycles – in perfect balance.

This essence addresses the needy child within us and the dynamic of Balance – helping to restore, through adequate nurture, the equilibrium point between self denial and excessive hunger (both emotional and physical) – neediness and denial of needs, dissatisfaction and greed, famine and feast, bitterness and sweetness etc. Its healing lies in re-uniting us with the archetypal strong caring mother in our psyche – filling that part of the void, which in spiritual terms we created when we separated, and which in terms of human experience has arisen out of inadequate or excessive mothering or smothering.

Both inadequate and excessive mothering can leave our child self in a state of arrested development and we need the energetic experience of the strong wise empowering mother to replace the early matrix so that our inner child can be sufficiently loved and encouraged to enable it to grow up with the ability to nurture, support and empower itself throughout life.

In terms of the world at present its purpose is to address the void and insecurity in the hearts and guts of humanity – the fear of lack of love, nurture and support. Heart Mother also addresses our relationship with the earth (the mother), and the management, use and sacredness of the earth's resources as well as of our own.

In terms of men who rape, this essence addresses the bitterness and void in their hearts arising from rejection and lack of love and nurture from their own mother. This bitterness, deep anger and empty hunger is re-played in their relationships with other women.

Heart Mother also looks at how much we mother others and create a role for ourselves as a 'helper' as a subconscious way of filling the void within ourselves. It encourages us to look at how this relationship with others is disabling to them, and it inspires us to look at what empowers others to find their own answers and their own strength and capability. This essence encourages mothers and male or female carers, to 'get a life' for themselves as individuals, separate to their identity as wives, mothers, male carers or house husbands.

As mothers, this essence encourages us to 'cut the apron strings', and to empower our children to go out into the world, to learn from their experiences and from the 'mistakes' they make. It helps us to not 'pick up the pieces' or carry things for them (both literally and emotionally), but to be there for them to reflect back to them their own integrity, capability and potential.

See also: Cyclamen, Pussy Willow, Inner Fire, Red Poppy, Blue Delphinium, Pure Love, Physostegia, Father Sun, Goldenrod, Grandmothers Arms.

Honesty

Lunaria anuua

"This above all: to thine own self be true and it must follow, as the night the day, thou canst not then be false to any man" William Shakespeare (Hamlet)

"To be honest with others about who you are, to speak your truth, is to be vulnerable. Vulnerability is the most powerful place of being. It is that place where there can be no dissension. It is also the most fearful place for many of you, because you fear judgement. You fear that if you open your heart, someone will put a knife in it.

The reality is that when you speak forth your truth, you are really allowing the merging of hearts to take place because vulnerability is irresistible. When you find that there is truly nothing to defend, your ego has taken a back seat and your heart is driving you to a place of non-separation".

P'taah "The Gift" channelled by Jani King

Indications: Hiding our true feelings, or the truth about a situation, from oneself or from others for fear of judgement; for sensitivity to criticism or judgement from others; fear of exposure; for when one's honesty is questioned; for when we feel misjudged and misunderstood; for when we deceive ourselves and others in order to protect ourselves from judgement; for when we feel threatened when others around us express their true feelings or the truth about a situation; for when we deny our truth in an attempt to live according to the standards of others or of society; for when we work hard to maintain an image of perfection in order to hide our vulnerability; for stage fright.

Honesty shows us that it is our deep yearning for love, and our fear of being denied that love, which motivates us to hide the truth of who we are from ourselves and from others. We fear honesty because we fear judgement – believing in some way that we are not 'good enough' by our own standards or by the standards of others, and believing that our human-ness might be seen as an expression of imperfection.

Honesty encourages us to embrace and own our true feelings and the truth about our actions, with love and understanding and without judgement. In this way, even our anger can be expressed with love and responsibility for ourselves and for our integrity, rather than as an attack against others. Our 'negative' feelings are simply cries from our heart, showing us the ways in which we have denied our integrity, been unloving towards ourselves, or perhaps projected our pain onto others. When we recognise this, we need no longer fear our painful feelings, recognising them simply as our hearts' call for love and integrity.

Honesty encourages us to open our hearts to ourselves and to others, without fear of judgement. It helps us to become self-knowing – to lovingly understand what motivates our actions, and to recognise that whilst we continue to judge ourselves, we will continue to attract those who will mirror our judgement of ourselves back to us. When we unconditionally embrace and understand our feelings, and understand how they motivate our actions, we no longer feel crushed by the judgements of others. We begin to feel able to honestly express our feelings, admit our 'mistakes' and show our human-ness and vulnerability, knowing that this expression of truth is a gift of love to the world. In so doing, we inspire others around us to relax and to feel undefended enough to show their essential human-ness too.

See also: Original Innocence, Loving Me – Loving You, Blue Delphinium, Red Quince, Red Deadnettle, Heart Flow, Phoenix Rebirth, Blue Salvia, Crab Apple Fruit, Goldenrod, Red Gladiolus, Orange Wallflower, Pure Love, True Power, Violet, Physostegia, Red Poppy.

Horse Chestnut Leaf Bud

Aesculus hippocastanum

Indications: for whenever we (both men and women) are reluctant to embrace our masculine, yang energy; for men who lack confidence in their physicality, sexuality or virility; for men who are uncomfortable with some aspect of their physicality and sexual expression, perhaps because of past experiences or because of cultural or religious influences; for women who feel 'turned off' sex in some way, or who are uncomfortable with some aspect of male physicality and sexuality.

❄

Horse Chestnut Leaf Bud essence relates to whenever we are reluctant, (as men or women), to appreciate or to embrace our masculine, yang energy, or a more yang, pro-active, assertive way of being and relating. We may have witnessed this masculine yang energy being used to dominate and control others and are therefore reluctant to appreciate or to embody that kind of energy in our relationships, or in our way of relating to the world. Horse Chestnut Leaf Bud inspires us to embody and use our masculine, yang energy with love and respect for own integrity, and for the integrity of others.

Horse Chestnut Leaf Bud also celebrates the wonderful Pan-like energy of male physicality and sexuality, the tree-like beauty of men's bodies and the thrusting power of their sensuality and sexuality, seeking receptivity, deep embrace and unconditional transcendental communion.

Many men have mixed and unresolved feelings about their body and their sexuality, perhaps because of past experiences, peer group pressure and judgements, past rejection by partners, or as a result of the pervasive influence of media, cultural or religious attitudes. Horse Chestnut Leaf Bud inspires a love and deep understanding of male sexual energy, and the male body. It inspires men to reconnect with love, to the beauty and potency of their male sensuality and sexuality, and to give the gift of that male beauty with love and tenderness, and with respect for their own and their partner's integrity.

This essence also inspires women to love and appreciate male physicality and sexuality. For those women who feel turned off sex in some way, who seek union on emotional, mental or spiritual levels but are not necessarily comfortable with physical union, this essence can provide the 'missing link', inspiring a relaxed and humorous attraction to male physicality and sexuality, a real enjoyment and pleasure in lovemaking and 'good sex', and an understanding of the energy and dynamics of male sexuality.

There is much that remains to be healed and understood in relation to our experience of human sexuality. As with all other areas of our experience there is a call for love, compassion, and integrity in our journey of healing and understanding. For this reason, when addressing issues around sexuality we may also need to look at the following areas of our experience:

our feelings in relation to female sexuality, and in relation to our original choice to enter a sexual relationship with another – *Red Gladiolus*;

our fear of speaking out – *Blue Delphinium*;

our need to set boundaries and be true to ourselves – *Red Poppy, Physostegia, Phoenix Rebirth and Goldenrod*;

the pain of past rejection – *Red Deadnettle*;

our guilt and our need to forgive ourselves and others – *Original Innocence and Phoenix Rebirth*;

our fear of exposure, our dislike of our body, or our fear of intimacy – *Honesty, Heart Flow and Loving Me, Loving Me, Loving You*;

our judgement of others – *Beauty in the Eye and Yellow Hyacinth*;

our fear of letting go and losing control – *Letting Go*;

our co-dependency – *Pure Love*.

Inner Fire

Inner Warrior Essence

Energetic signature of fire agate, fire-pit, south red sandstone & eagle's feather

Indications: for when we need the courage, clarity and strength to bring an end to a situation that is no longer tolerable; for when we find ourselves repeatedly feeling powerless and frustrated; for whenever we need to set clear boundaries and put our foot down; for strong, peaceful assertion; for the base and solar plexus chakras.

✳

For embodying the warrior within: for inner power – embodying the inner masculine; for gathering our inner energy and fire; for courage, strength, clarity, accurate vision, discernment and powerful decisive action; for embodying the fire of truth and rekindling the flames of certainty and strength.

Inner Fire helps us when we feel that we do not have the strength, courage and clarity to take empowered action. It inspires us with certainty of truth and clear vision to be in our power, to stand firmly for what is right in any given situation, to set boundaries, to build and maintain a core of energy and strength, and to direct and use our energy and fire accurately and efficiently as needed.

Often this essence arises when we need bring a situation to an end, or when we need to draw a line in the sand. We may previously have found it hard to stand our ground and to say no because we have felt unable to muster enough strength and certainty behind what we were saying for our voice to be heard and honoured.

Inner Fire helps us to gather sufficient fire energy and clarity to take accurate, decisive and effective action. In this way we are able to say "Enough is enough!" – and our words are now heard and respected and our actions are successful. Inner Fire embodies qualities of both the warrior and the hunter, who need clear sight, accurate timing and decisive action to bring about a swift, clean end, without mess and without need for further action.

If we have been brought up in a polite environment in which people did not express directly what they were feeling, where anger was taboo or was suppressed, or used subversively in manipulative behaviour, then we may never have learnt to call a spade a spade, and may be afraid to be clear and unequivocal. Inner Fire inspires us to realise that we have a basic human right to stand fully in our power. We all have a right to do this, and by doing so we free up the energy of many situations and bring clarity and strength to our interactions. Where there is fear of speaking out it may be helpful to combine Inner Fire with Blue Delphinium.

Inner Fire, Blue Delphinium, Phoenix Rebirth and Cherry Plum Fruit can be used whenever we repeatedly explode our anger onto those around us in violent outbursts. This combination encourages us to embrace our feelings with understanding and without reaction and inspires us to find ways to peacefully and effectively express our feelings and assert ourselves, instead of resorting to violence or intimidation.

When we are afraid of our masculine power and fire, because we have seen how that fire can be used to dominate others, we can combine Inner Fire with Horse Chestnut Leaf Bud and True Power, so that we may learn how to use our masculine fire with love, and with respect for our own integrity and the integrity of others. Where we are afraid of judgement, Inner Fire can be combined with Goldenrod, Honesty and Physostegia. When we are afraid to show our anger because we don't want to jeopardise a relationship, we can combine Inner Fire with Pure Love.

Inner Fire is a powerful fire essence and I do not recommend that it be used on it's own for longer than 5 days at a time. When combined with other essences, I would suggest it be taken for no more than a month, with at least a month's break before using again, otherwise one can become very driven, unrelaxed and fiery. For longer term use, to address issues of anger and powerlessness, I would recommend Red Poppy, used either on its own or in combination with other essences.

See also: With Love, Blue Delphinium, Blue Salvia, Phoenix Rebirth, Original Innocence, Cherry Plum Fruit, Heart Mother, At the Heart of Being, Physostegia, Goldenrod, True Power, Red Quince Red Deadnettle and Crimean Snowdrop.

Letting Go

Hyacinthus 'White Pearl'

"Leap, and the net will appear"

Indications: fear of letting go of the 'security' of old fears, beliefs and limited perceptions of ourselves and of life; fear of change, fear of losing control; for letting go of deep fears that arise in the human psyche at times of transformation; fear of letting go at the point of dying; for when we hang on to old fears by our fingernails and toes; fear of letting go of built up emotion, old hurts, grudges and resentments or people that we are clinging to.

Letting Go encourages us to step into the light and joy of divine reality. Over many, centuries, we have created and maintained a limited view of who we are, of what the world consists of and of how it works. Now, at this time, we are entering a period of profound transformation and change, in which we are repeatedly challenged at every level of our experience, to let go of old beliefs and perceptions and to step forward into a divine experience and perception of life. We are being called upon to let go, and let go, and let go, into an ever expanding and deepening multi-dimensional experience of being.

There are times when we hold back and cling on to the old, afraid to move on from the security and limitation of the known, into the world of the unknown. This essence reassures us that we are not alone as we step forward into what seems like uncharted territory. It reminds us that we are constantly partnered by spiritual companions, who walk with us and rejoice whenever we let go and let the expanded vision of God/Good support us and lead us into the light.

It is easy to forget when we come up against our deepest fears, that we are facing an opportunity to move into a wonderful and expanded experience of ourselves and of life. We would not have reached this point of transformation, if we had not outgrown the restriction of our previous 'caterpillar' form. Letting Go helps us to realize, that like the butterfly emerging from its chrysalis, we too are on the verge of flying free into a wonderful, expanded experience of ourselves and of the world. It helps us to understand that our fears are illusory and unnecessary – that the little voice in our ear, undermining our confidence, is telling us lies. The voice for fear always says "What if" and never tells us what is.

Letting Go relates to whenever we are afraid to let go, whether that letting go be of fear, anger, bitterness, emotional build up, people we have clung onto, or accumulated tension resulting from the effort of trying to control our world out of fear. It reassures us that it is safe to let go, and to allow ourselves to bask in the infinite peace and safety of divine being – that we will be supported, and we will find a safety net appearing, once we have stopped clinging on so desperately, and have finally let go.

See also: Living the Dream, Red Clover, Stitchwort, Child's Play, Divine Being, White Yarrow, Pussy Willow, Lilac, Reunion, Crimean Snowdrop, Phoenix Rebirth, Cherry Plum Fruit, Sweet Pea, Passionate Life.

Lilac

Syringa vulgaris

Indications: for complex work and study situations; for whenever we feel overwhelmed by the complexity of information that we are studying, or the complexity of a project; for when we don't know how to manage and structure a multi-dimensional, complex project or organisation; for discomfort with chaos and complexity; for when we have so many confusing issues confronting us, we don't know where to begin.

❄

Lilac helps us to steer an instinctive path through complex information and situations. Faced with complicated information or a mass of tasks, it helps us to find an intuitive starting point, inspiring us to find a more lateral, right-brained approach to dealing with complexity and multi-level, multi-dimensional situations or information.

Faced with complexity and chaos, our rational, linear left-brain tends to panic and freeze, or to want to regiment and order things. Whilst this is appropriate in some situations, in others it may limit the unfolding development of a project, or of our understanding. Responsiveness to new understanding or to better ways of doing things – and open-ness to change and creative inspiration, are restricted if we try to rigidly structure the way that we approach complexity and chaos.

An intuitive approach to chaos and complexity allows for all the many pieces of information and aspects of a project, to evolve and come together, bit by bit in what may seem a completely random fashion when viewed from close up. If we are working on an in-depth and complex creative project in this way, there may be many factors that feed into the project. Chance encounters whilst shopping, books read, a programme on the radio, a conversation with a friend, a challenging issue, or a Eureka moment whilst walking, may all bring new links, new ideas, new connections or information – sometimes crucial to the actual success of the project.

When we allow it to, all of life may feed into a project and greatly enrich it. It is like looking at a detailed, complex tapestry. From close up, it appears as though we are just creating a random mass of different stitches and colours. As we move further away, the detail and dimensions of the pattern emerges.

In a sense this is how the creation of this book evolved, like a multi-dimensional tapestry, over a period of two years – inextricably interwoven and interlinked with the pattern and unfolding of events in my life and in the world. Inspiration and insight fed into this writing from many sources: from watching, listening, and mulling things over; from challenging issues; past experience and notebooks; from working with clients; and from profound cranio-sacral therapy and journey work. I drew on inspiring books and conversations; listened to the news(!); went for long walks; learnt from the richness of family life and wrote with an overall sense of a shared journey with friends in spirit. Lilac inspired this whole process – that and the decision to take my time and to enjoy the whole journey as it unfolded.

The timing in which various parts, or the whole of a project comes together will be far more appropriate if it is not fixed by rigid mental deadlines. Unrealistic, short deadlines can mean that corners are cut, things are not thought through properly in enough depth, ideas are not given time to develop, or to be tested. The most opportune timing for the launch of a project is not always something that can be engineered. A thing is ready, when it is ready, and often it is worth the wait, because that extra care and attention to detail, in the end, may reap dividends An intuitive arrival at a launch date, may be far more spot on in terms of market readiness, than a calculated and rushed launch.

Key inspirational thinkers in management and organisational approaches at this time – such as Margaret Wheatley and Myron Keller-Rogers (see Suggested Reading p.257), inspire organisations to find more flexible, responsive, web-like ways of organising themselves – ways that encourage interacting communication and contribution from all levels of the workforce, a constant sharing and development of ideas, and the ability to rapidly and creatively respond to change, or to problems. They describe the way life organises itself naturally, and the inherent patterns formed out of seeming chaos – as seen in the unfolding multi-dimensional patterns of fractals. They talk about how creative systems evolve and self-organise naturally and appropriately, when allowed to, how the whole of life is interconnected, and how everything affects everything else.

In terms of the ongoing evolution of a project or an organisation, this awareness encourages us to allow many factors to feed into that process: the well-being of all those involved; the observations and creative ideas of those involved at every level; lessons learnt from overcoming challenges and problems; multi-cultural influences; new ideas that excite, inspire or are fun; information from the worldwide web; local influences; ecological and environmental factors; sustainability; educational factors etc. From the perspective of Lilac – influences, information and inspiration, come from many sources – both from outside, as well as from within an organisation. If we allow and encourage this process, we also encourage a fertile, creative, interactive environment, which embraces change and evolution as part of the natural process of living.

Lilac often arises when we face a confusing mass of issues. We may feel overwhelmed by all that needs sorting in our lives, unsure about where to begin – or too daunted even to start, because we are afraid of how long it will take to sort out everything we are facing. (This dynamic could equally well apply to children faced with the prospect of tidying their bedrooms, or to students revising!) Sometimes we are impatient and want to deal with everything at once, and want to get everything sorted as fast as possible.

In these situations Lilac shows us where to begin, and then what to deal with next, and next and next. It encourages us to have the patience, and the trust in ourselves and in life, to follow the process through, as it unfolds and begins to form a picture that makes sense and enlightens us. It may take time, or it may be a lot quicker and easier than we think. If we combine Lilac with Speedwell and Comfrey, we may enjoy the richness of our journey far better, embracing all the things we discover, that inspire and enlighten us along the way.

See also: Speedwell, Pussy Willow, Comfrey, Golden Blessings, The Rose, Reunion, Living the Dream, Disciple of the Heart, With Love, Sweet Hunza.

Living the Dream

Inspirational Light Essence

Indications: for whenever we do not fully trust that it is possible to live our vision for ourselves and for the world; for when we waver, doubt, or lose hope of realising our dreams; for when we dream but hold back from taking positive steps to manifest our dreams.

Living the Dream brings positive affirmation that profound change is upon us now. It says that from now on the reality of divine being will be experienced as concrete fact, if we choose to affirm it in our perception of ourselves and of life.

It takes us far beyond trust and hope, into empowerment and positive action that affirms our choice to create heaven on earth, now, at this time. 'Living the Dream' affirms that love does prevail and it shows us that our peaceful assertion of the reality of love, can heal the world and our experience of ourselves and of life. Through this assertion we form the basis of how the world will operate from now on, and through it we create peace, healing, and joy.

Living the Dream helps us to remember our soul incarnation choice at this time and to become clearer in our vision of where we are going, even if we do not necessarily know how we will get there. It moves us from being the dreamer, to *living* the dream and it strengthens the integration of the Higher Self, enabling us to know, with greater accuracy when and how to act, in order to manifest our dreams into reality.

This essence confirms that love, peace, healing, joy and abundance are our birthright. It strengthens within us the union of courage with knowing – knowing that love works. It encourages us in our own personal journey of healing and supports us in making peaceful positive choices to create a new reality for ourselves and for the world.

See also: Pussy Willow, Child's Play, With Love, Disciple of the Heart, Cyclamen, Red Poppy, Stitchwort, Golden Blessings, Passionate Life.

Loving Me, Loving You

Erica cinerea

"What we embrace transforms"

Indications: For when we are dissatisfied with ourselves and judge ourselves to be somehow not good enough as we are; for low self-worth and lack of confidence – when we dislike some aspect of ourselves and want to be different from how we are now – thinner, cleverer, more beautiful, more successful, younger, older or more experienced; for when we compare ourselves favourably or unfavourably to others; when we are un-relaxed and self-conscious around others, afraid that someone will see behind our front to how we really are; when we are obsessed with image or with 'bettering' ourselves, when we project our judgment of ourselves onto those around us, judging others and wanting them to be different or 'better' in some way.

Loving Me, Loving You encourages us to embrace and love ourselves just as we are, right now – to feel relaxed and happy with who we are – not needing to be different in any way to how we truly are. It inspires us to have compassion and understanding for ourselves and for others – to embrace with love and laughter all our 'imperfections', to celebrate our uniqueness, and to settle joyfully into being who we are, whether we are tall or short, fat or thin, dark or fair, enlightened or un-enlightened, clever or not, tidy or untidy, successful or not – however we are, this essence encourages us to be happy to be real, to accept and to show our human-ness, to laugh at ourselves and life, and to be warm and loving towards ourselves and towards others.

Society, media, advertising, in addition to many religions and spiritual practices, promote the idea that we will only be loved or blessed if we live up to some perfect image or ideal. As a consequence of this, even if we try hard not to listen to these suggestions, we often feel inadequate in some way and attempt to change, or to hide these supposed 'imperfections' from others, fearing that we will not be loved unless we become more 'perfect' than we currently perceive ourselves to be.

This is a no-win game that often takes us down the route of self-hatred, guilt, obsession with weight, or with 'improving' ourselves in some way, or of perhaps trying to create and maintain a perfect house, garden, family or spiritual practice. No matter how wonderful we may appear on the outside – we may be the thinnest, cleverest, most beautiful, fit, successful or enlightened person in the world – if we don't really love ourselves, warts and all, we will live in constant fear of our 'perfect' image slipping and of love being withdrawn.

The true fact of the matter is, that when we love and fully embrace who we are, and the reality of our life, with warmth and laughter, we spread love and acceptance to all around us, no matter what our shape, size or aptitude – everyone around us feels relaxed, embraced and joyful in our company, because we are real and happy with our real-ness, and honour what is real in others.

Loving Me, Loving You, releases us from the tyranny of image and shows us the beauty of being real – of showing our true face and our true beauty. True beauty arises from within our own hearts, from the radiance of the love that we give to ourselves and that we radiate out into the world. When we relax and drop our image and our front and show our real self and our real feelings to the world, with love and with laughter, we liberate others to begin to relax and be brave enough to show their human-ness and real-ness too.

See also: Beauty in the Eye, Yellow Hyacinth, With Love, Original Innocence, Golden Blessings. Disciple of the Heart, Honesty, Horse Chestnut Leaf Bud, The Rose

One Being

Medicine Man Quartz

"While I stood there, I saw more than I can tell, and I understood more than I saw; for I was seeing in a sacred manner the shape of all things in the spirit, and the shape of all shapes as they must live together as one being"

– Black Elk

Indications: for deepening meditation and attunement; for development of true clairvoyant and clairaudient awareness through meditation and attunement; for whenever we feel disconnected from the world and from divine awareness of the world and wish to deepen our connection and communion with devas, spirits, people, plants, animals, the natural world and environments we are working within.

For 'being' still – living meditation. For being deeply centred, fully present – at one with oneself and with the One Being in all. Deep peace – deep connection to divine Being; for meditation, attunement, development of true clairvoyance and clairaudience. (One Being is one of four essences that combine to create the "At One" meditation combination).

For settling into the undisturbed stillness and peace of our fully conscious being – experiencing the infinite peace of the one 'Being' – the vital hum (Aum) of the divine in all. For no longer identifying with a limited mortal sense of 'self' and 'other', or with the illusory emotional waves of the fearful ego.

One Being can be used for meditation, connection, attunement and the ongoing development of true clairvoyant and clairaudient abilities. By stilling the mind and emotions, and being 'at one' with people, environments, the natural world and animals, without reaction or ego judgement, we can develop a more accurate extrasensory perception and awareness of what is true, and when appropriate, be able to see more clearly how we might act for the greater benefit of all.

This essence can also be used for those who feel isolated and cut off from the world outside themselves; who, perhaps as a result of illness or other circumstances, are unable to actively participate in the world and feel as though they exist in a disconnected vacuum. Through stillness One Being connects us powerfully to the presence and spirit of the one in all – to the unity of all people and all beings, to rain falling on leaves, the language of birdsong, the presence of trees, the miniature world of insects and small creatures, the vitality of the air we breathe.

One Being resonates with the depth of communion and clear vision of the elder medicine people of this world and with their communion with the spirits of the land, the plants, the animals and the people. It also connects us to our own universal Buddha awareness. We may draw on this essence to further our connection and understanding of the natural world, and for whenever we are working with devas, spirits, people, plants, animals or environments, to commune more clearly with them, and to understand better their condition and the reality of any situation.

One Being teaches us to combine clear vision with respect for the spirit and life role of each being and each place, without prejudice, and to honour and to understand when it is (with permission), or is not appropriate for us to play a role in promoting the healing of an individual or an environment.

I had a most profound experience while making this essence. I have never found sitting meditation easy, having always been very restless. The closest I had got to regular meditation was whilst walking alone. I had long wanted to sustain the stillness and connection that I had experienced occasionally whilst meditating. On the morning of the day I made this essence, I had cancelled my place on a workshop that was being run by a friend who is a wonderful and experienced clairvoyant. I had wanted to go to his workshop in order to further develop my clairvoyant, clairaudient and clairsentient abilities and I was disappointed at having to cancel, although I knew that it was the right decision at the time.

What I found very moving about the creation of One Being was the realisation that through this essence I had been given this gift of 'living' meditation, and that through this depth of connection and communion, true clairvoyance, clairaudience and clairsentience are developed. It was as though "when one door closes another opens"- having given up the workshop I was given another way to come to my heart's desire, but from the inside out and I am grateful for that.

One Being was made over twenty four hours, in my garden using a large chunk of creamy yellowish quartz that looks in profile like the face of a North American native elder, or a Thai Buddha. I found this stone many years ago outside a disused silver and lead mine in Wales. On the first morning of making this essence as I was driving into town a barn owl appeared and floated in front of the windscreen of my car as I drove down our small road. Twice it flew up to sit on the branch above me in the middle of the road. Each time I stopped my car and we looked at each other for some time before he took off again to glide once more in front of the car. This continued for half a mile until the owl flew off into a field on my right. Owls, and particularly barn owls often appear and fly beside my car at times when I am moving into deeper awareness in my work and in my life. I always feel honoured and supported by their presence as though they are messengers from spirit bringing confirmation of what I am doing and what I feel is happening.

In the evening of that same day, I sat in our garden, not far from where the essence was being made and found myself entering into an experience of complete and profound stillness and connection – at one with everything around me in the garden and the universe. This experience lasted uninterrupted for over an hour, at the end of which I was overwhelmed by the beauty and depth of this connection. Since that evening this stillness and connection has stayed with me as though I am in more of a state of 'living' meditation as I move through the world.

See also: Rosebay Willowherb, At the Heart of Being, Reunion, Speedwell, Lilac, Comfrey, Sky Blue Comfrey.

Orange Wallflower

Cheiranthus cheirii

Indications: for loneliness; neediness; insecurity about relationships; co-dependency; for fear of love being withheld or denied; feeling an outsider; feeling on the edge of groups or of society; fear of lack of love or lack of abundance; for whenever we block the flow of giving and receiving because of fear.

For becoming one's own best friend; for learning how to like, support and appreciate ourselves; for being comfortable with ourselves; for experiencing the deep well of love and friendship that lies within us, that we can draw on at any time to embrace and support ourselves; for knowing that there is no lack of love or abundance, that love can never be diminished, except in our perception.

Orange Wallflower is an essence that relates to our first steps in becoming secure in love and appreciation of ourselves. It addresses the insecurity that often arises from our first childhood attempts at making friends and socialising in group situations away from the security and support of home. Often our first childhood social experiences influence how relaxed we as adults now feel about ourselves in group situations and how easily, or not, we are able to make and maintain friendships. This essence is useful when a child first goes to nursery or playgroup, or starts a new school, but equally it applies to healing the wounds that we as adults still carry from those first encounters.

Orange Wallflower addresses when we feel lonely and awkward in group situations – when we feel different – the outsider – when we don't feel embraced or accepted as a member of a community, or of society in general, and when we are not confident in forming one to one friendships with our peers. It helps us when we are afraid that others will not want to get to know us, and when we desperately long for friendship and inclusion. Orange Wallflower teaches us that friendship begins at home in our own hearts, in our enjoyment of our own unique company, and that it is our lack of confidence and our neediness that energetically makes other people feel awkward and un-relaxed around us, and that leaves us feeling the 'wallflower at the party.'

Orange Wallflower brings the sweet warmth of self-appreciation to our hearts, helping us to really like and enjoy our own company and our unique being. It teaches us how to be a good and loving friend towards ourselves and shows us that we have within us a boundless source of love and friendship, a source that never runs dry, and on which we can draw at any time.

The Doctrine of Signatures of the plant from which this essence is made, reflects the qualities of the essence. This wallflower grows out from between the bricks of our crumbling garden wall. There is almost no mortar in this wall, and certainly no soil or obvious nutrients, let alone any moisture. Each year, for many years, this solitary plant has grown bigger and bigger, creating an abundance of branches covered in a rich mass of sweetly scented deep orange flowers. It is as though it draws its nourishment from the air itself – as though it knows no lack, only abundance of all its needs. When I made this essence I heard sung the words "Love is in the Air" from the song of that name.

See also: Red Deadnettle, Pure Love, Living the Dream, Physostegia, Honesty, Heart Flow, Blue Delphinium, Heart Mother, Father Sun, Cyclamen and Red Quince.

Original Innocence

Indications: deep feelings of guilt, failure and unworthiness; self-punishment; never feeling good enough; taking on guilt or responsibility that doesn't belong to one; self-hatred; believing we are unworthy of love, or cannot reach heaven or enlightenment unless we become perfect and pure.

Original Innocence addresses the deep feelings of guilt, unworthiness and imperfection that have arisen in the human psyche since the time of separation from our Divine Being. It inspires us to realise that all that stands between us, and our experiencing the true light and perfection of our divine being – are our judgemental thoughts that continually tell us that we are unworthy and that we will never be good enough. It also addresses our perception that enlightenment and the realisation of divine being, is only attained by those who reach some ideal of purity and perfection.

The simple realisation of Original Innocence is that we are already perfect every moment of our being. We do not need to prove anything to ourselves or to anyone else in order to experience the perfection of who we are right now. It shows us that our judgemental thoughts are just that – judgemental thoughts. By our judgement we repeatedly set ourselves up for failure, striving to reach unreal, unloving goals and false images of perfection that we frequently fall short of achieving. By these judgements we hold ourselves separate from the love in our hearts and from the experience of our ever-present good.

Now is the time to release ourselves and others from centuries of false unloving judgement that has kept us within the limitation of 'sinners', and never 'good enough'. When we cease judging ourselves and others, all our actions become motivated by love. All the unloving actions in the world have arisen from the pain of separation from our Love, and from our true, divine perfection. It is the often unrecognised pain of self-judgement, of not feeling 'good enough', of feeling unworthy of love and unworthy of good, that has driven people to harming themselves and others, and that has led to the false pursuit of 'power'.

For many of us, the point at which we turn on others and judge them, is the point at which we ourselves feel that we have done 'wrong'. In our pain of self-judgement we may attempt to make another person appear 'wrong', in order to distract ourselves and others from our own 'wrongdoing'. For some, this turning point of guilt and shame is also the point at which we sink into destructive or self-destructive behaviour, as though we feel: "Well I've messed up anyway – I'm no good and never will be – I might as well mess up big time – who cares?"

It is our self-judgement and the judgement of others that has kept us from realising the essential ever-present divine perfection of all beings. Original Innocence encourages us to wipe the slate clean – to allow our experience to be constantly one of ever-new, completely innocent beginnings, untainted by former actions and judgements. In this way we continually move on, with no weight of the past holding us back in guilt and patterns that we need to move on from.

When we connect with our true innocence we begin to understand our actions with great love and compassion and can learn from them. Original Innocence helps us to purify our perception, so that we can constantly see ourselves and others in the light of our true innocence. It reminds us too that what we believe about ourselves, the world reflects back to us: if we judge ourselves, we will find ourselves judged. When we let go of the guilt and judgement in our perception, we experience ourselves and others in our true form.

This essence relates to the time of the 'Fall' – when we originally chose to separate from the experience of ourselves as divine. The further we grew in memory from our divinity, the more we perceived ourselves and others to be 'less than' whole – less than divine. Divinity began to be seen as something out of reach of mere mortals, rather than the essence of ourselves and of all that is. We also began to see this planet as separate from the divine and gradually we lost our sense of one-ness with the divine in all things and all beings, here on earth.

Out of this forgetfulness we developed religions, worshipping the divine as something separate from who we were. Some of these religions instilled the perception that we are sinners – tainted by Original Sin, and guilty of being 'less than' divine. Many preached a fear of holy judgement by some stern God, setting strict tenets to live by in order to strive towards a seemingly unreachable perfection. Holiness and enlightenment were seen as achievable by only a few select and special beings. The earth became seen as a godless temporary abode for sinners or for those still treading the wheel of Karma.

Through the promulgation and re-inforcement of guilt, judgement, and ideas of perfection, we have allowed ourselves and others to be controlled over aeons of time. We ourselves may have increased our sense of power and attempted to control others in this way. Hierarchies and power structures have been created and maintained through ideas of superiority and perfection. This has kept nations and whole worlds within a sense of limitation and inferiority and has strengthened false power structures. This non-realisation of the divine and of Love has not only been played out on this planet but also in other arenas of the universe and multi-verses.

As each of us awakens to the realisation of our true innocent perfection, and to the power of love and truth, the veil of illusion thins, allowing for more of the light of divine truth to shine through, thus quickening a wider awakening and healing. It is now time to stand in the light of our divine innocent Being – to free ourselves and the earth from the chains of judgement and guilt that have kept us within a sense of limitation and imperfection for so long.

See also: True Power, Phoenix Rebirth, Yellow Hyacinth, Crab Apple Fruit, Heart Flow, Red Poppy, Loving Me – Loving You, Disciple of the Heart and Pink Cherry.

Passionate Life

Amaryllis belladonna with Apophyllite, pale Amethyst and clear Quartz crystals

Indications: for whenever we need a boost to our courage and confidence; for fear of risks and challenges; for lack of confidence and motivation; discouragement, disheartenment, hopelessness; feeling a victim of circumstance; fear of living; timidity; being over-protective of oneself; living a narrow existence out of fear;

❋

The positive qualities of Passionate Life are: energy, enthusiasm, courage, joy, adventurousness, motivation, zest for life and new experiences; being passionately alive; overcoming obstacles and setbacks; rebuilding confidence and resilience after illness and setbacks.

Passionate Life relates to the flow of fire energy in our life, and to the degree in which we inhibit our fire energy, and our drive out of fear. There are many reasons why we hold back from adventure and challenge. Sometimes it is out of fear of failure, other times we are afraid of putting ourselves at risk. Fundamental to our fear is a sense of powerlessness, a lack of trust in ourselves and our abilities, a fear of not being in control, and a lack of trust in being supported in our venture into the unknown.

Passionate Life helps us to understand the frightened child inside us, so that we can identify why we are afraid. Sometimes we don't yet feel ready to take on a challenge – in which case we may need to work on developing our abilities, our confidence, our resourcefulness and our survival skills, until we feel more capable of looking after ourselves and tackling new adventures. Drawing on the support of Passionate Life combined with Wild Cyclamen, we can help our inner child grow up, so that it can become more confident and capable, and more trusting in itself and in the continuing support of spiritual guides and companions.

It may be that we don't trust our fire energy. Perhaps in the past we have become over fired up and over-enthusiastic about a project, and have not grounded our fire energy enough, and have therefore been irresponsible or ineffective in our actions, or have quickly burnt out. As a result, we no longer trust our fire energy and our ability to manage it without harming ourselves or others. If we grew up with a parent whose fire energy was unpredictable and unstable – who was prone to wild, childish enthusiasm and big ungrounded projects – we may have developed a more serious, responsible adult persona to counter the irresponsibility of our parent. As an adult now, we may be afraid of enthusiasm and adventurousness because it reminds us of the damaging effect of our parent's instability, which we do not want to reproduce in our own lives.

By combining Passionate Life with Cherry Plum Fruit, Wild Cyclamen, Child's Play, Heart Mother and Speedwell, we can begin to learn to play, and to trust ourselves to become more adventurous in our own way, and in our own timing. In this way we learn how to stay centred and confident whilst venturing into new territory.

When are holding back from new challenges out of fear of failure, the Bach Remedy Larch can be used on an ongoing basis, together with Passionate Life and Wild Cyclamen. If we are afraid of putting ourselves at risk, particularly with physical adventure or travelling, we may wish to combine Passionate Life with Green Alexanders, Red Clover and Speedwell.

Passionate Life helps us to muster the courage to 'have a go' at doing something new. How fast we move out of familiar territory is up to us. By taking Passionate Life we can uncover where our resistance lies, and by combining it with other essences, we can gradually develop the confidence in ourselves and in life, to really begin to explore new areas of life and new experiences.

See also: Heart Mother, Red Clover, Wild Cyclamen, Living the Dream, Green Alexanders, Red Poppy, Letting Go, Stitchwort, Child's Play, Speedwell, Father Sun, Sweet Pea, Cherry Plum Fruit.

Peaceful Detachment

Achillea millefolium

Indications: for over-empathy, oversensitivity to, and over-involvement with the level of ego/emotional reactive drama in our own and other people's lives; for therapists and healers who are over-sensitive and over-empathic.

❄

Peaceful Detachment looks at what happens when we involve ourselves in the emotional dynamics of other people's experiences – whether they are people we know, or people and events portrayed in the media. This essence reminds us that empathy is not necessarily a helpful way to connect with other people. When we empathise with someone, we join with them on the level of their wound and their suffering. We involve ourselves in their suffering, instead of joining with them at the level of their wholeness – their true self. We may have grown up believing that by being empathic we are being kind to others, but often we dis-empower others and support their suffering when we are empathic.

This essence helps us to see beyond the level of the emotional story to the opportunity for healing that lies behind the story. It's particularly important that we don't buy into other people's pain and suffering. This doesn't mean that we can't be deeply compassionate, but we don't need to suffer another's pain – we each have our own journey and learning to unfold. It's important that we stop viewing each other as helpless victims in our lives, and instead begin to hold each other in the light and potential of our divine self. Peaceful Detachment helps us to see the bigger picture, and the bigger person. It reminds us that we've each chosen our life and our experiences precisely for the learning and enlightenment that is offered by those particular circumstances and dynamics.

The level of our wound – the level of suffering – is the astral level. This has been called 'The Plain of Illusions' – since all suffering is a denial and a separation from the experience of divine reality and wholeness. At this present time, the level of the astral is clearing as we move away from suffering, into a realisation of the divine. This is a conscious process of realisation, as a result of which we are witnessing an intensification of the illusion of suffering as it arises to be addressed and transformed in our experience. If we look at our own lives or listen to the news, we need to be aware of how we think about what is happening, as well as the way we talk about events. We need to be very aware at this time, of not giving energy to negative or fearful perceptions of what is happening in the world or to those around us.

Peaceful Detachment reminds us that that we are all powerful, divine, beings, and that we've created our experience at this time, precisely for the opportunity to embrace the reality of our divine being. None of us are victims of circumstance, and if we wish to empower and heal ourselves and others, we need to connect with what's happening at the level of divine awareness. When we no longer give energy to the level of the wound in others, we can hold them in the light of their highest potential and healing. When we hold others in the light of their whole being, we empower them to find the resources and understanding they need in order to deal with their present challenges. Whenever we connect to the level of the divine and to a divine perspective, we create an energy of safety and peace, and an enlightened, empowered space in which healing and transformation can occur. There are no limitations in the divine.

One of the truths we have half understood is that we are all one. At some workshops and gatherings, group hugs have become 'de rigueur'. For some of us this feels an unsafe and uncomfortable experience, particularly if we are sensitive to other people's emotional energy. Joining with others on the level of the emotions and personality, can make us feel unsafe because it opens us up to the level of other people's wounds, and highlights our own unfinished business. Peaceful Detachment teaches us how to connect safely with others at the level of the higher self, beyond the level of wounds and personality. At this level there is no need for defence and we are all One.

Some of our fear of connecting with other people's emotional energy comes from our acute sensitivity as children to the energy of those around us. We may have been affected, consciously or subconsciously, by other people's emotional reactivity. Peaceful Detachment helps us to separate out from other people's emotional energy and their story, so that we can see what is our stuff and what is theirs. In this way we are no longer so affected by what's going on with others. Peaceful Detachment is one of the essences that relate to cutting unhealthy emotional ties with others (see Suggested reading – 'Cutting the Ties that Bind' by Phyllis Crystal).

See also: Red Clover, Heart Mother, Physostegia, At the Heart of Being, Divine Being, Stitchwort, Letting Go, Comfrey, Sweet Hunza, Crimean Snowdrop, One Being, Living the Dream, Celandine.

Phoenix Rebirth

Ulex Europaeus

Indications: forgiveness; for when we need to forgive, and to let go our judgement of ourselves and of others; for personal and community relationships where there is much unresolved old anger, conflict, and retribution, which it seems impossible to let go of and forgive; for when we perceive ourselves to be the 'victim' in our relationship with another person.

Phoenix Rebirth was made from the flowers of Gorse. Gorse bushes provide the first stabilising shrub cover (on light coastal and heathland soils), in the natural process of regeneration and re-forestation, following forest clearance or fire. These spiny bushes provide a sheltering environment through which the young trees of silver birch and oak can grow. Gorse survives in very dry soils and hot conditions. Its deep, yellow, warmly scented flowers bloom from early spring to August, although one may find bushes in flower almost year-long. This has inspired the traditional saying: "When Gorse is out of bloom, kissing's out of season".

Phoenix Rebirth inspires us to heal our perception of ourselves and others, with deep understanding and compassion – to withdraw our judgement, and to nurture a new way of relating – a fresh start, based on compassion, understanding and mutual self-worth. It also encourages us to move out of patterns of powerlessness, and out of playing the role of 'victim'.

Often we most judge others when we lack understanding and compassion for ourselves. Sometimes we are afraid to heal our perception of ourselves and of others, because we do not wish to face the challenge of taking responsibility for our part in the picture, and because we may not wish to let go of seeing others as the 'hateful' perpetrators in the stories that we have co-created together. When we let go our judgement, we can no longer maintain a feeling of superiority in defence against another.

What we discover if we are prepared to look further than the role of victim and perpetrator is that often both parties share some of the same issues. In spiritual terms, all souls concerned have agreed to play out these roles together, precisely for the purpose of embracing greater compassion, understanding and integrity, and for developing greater awareness of the dynamics of these situations.

Phoenix Rebirth encourages us to let go our desire for justice. It helps us to not return to old habits of judgement, but to understand instead, that we choose situations and people who will provide us with opportunities to honour our integrity, set boundaries, release karma, and experience the unity and healing of unconditional love. It tells us that it is not necessary to muster vast amounts of forgiveness in order to cancel out what we feel has been a huge act committed against us. Forgiveness is simply the act of withdrawing the judgement that we hold against ourselves and against others.

As part of the forgiveness process, we also need to move away from casting ourselves in the role of powerless victim. To do so, we need to fully embrace our anger, and we need to learn how to peacefully and powerfully assert our human rights, honour our integrity, and set appropriate boundaries. This is the image of the Phoenix – one of being reborn through fire. In order to completely forgive, we need to go through the fire of our anger, to learn the lessons that it is teaching us, and we need to take positive steps to break out of patterns of powerlessness that arise within our current experience. This completes the cycle. In this way we need no longer recreate the reactive, repeated patterns from the past, and we release others from co-creating these patterns with us.

There is a scene in the film of J.K. Rowling's book 'Harry Potter and the Chamber of Secrets', where the phoenix, Faulkes weeps tears of compassion into a fatal wound in Harry's arm. At once the wound heals completely, and Harry's life is saved. When making this essence I felt a need to combine the two aspects of water and fire and also a need for the essence to inspire a balance of masculine and feminine energy and awareness. There was a clear need for healing from fire, and the need to go through the fire of our anger in order to emerge reborn, but there was also a need for tears of deep understanding and compassion, in order to heal the wounds of the past and to wipe the slate clean for all concerned. So it felt appropriate, that this essence was made overnight, and as it turned out – half in rain, and half in sun.

Brandon Bays, whose work and whose book 'The Journey', offers profound tools for healing our perceptions of ourselves and of others, outlines a forgiveness process called the 'Camp Fire Process'. This process can completely alter our understanding of the dynamics of relationships in which we have felt a victim – this might be our relationship with our parents or with someone else whom we may feel has crushed or abused us. The 'Camp Fire Process' provides a way to uncover the emotional wounds that lie behind our own past actions or reactions, and the actions or reaction of others. When we truly understand what was going on for all parties concerned, we can no longer continue to hold judgement against ourselves or against any others involved. Brandon has kindly agreed to my reproducing to 'Camp Fire Process' in this book (see Understanding, Forgiveness & the 'Camp Fire Process' pages 233–238), as well as Suggested Reading and Useful Addresses.

See also: Original Innocence, Blue Delphinium, Yellow Hyacinth, Red Deadnettle. Inner Fire, Red Quince, Red Poppy, Honesty, Goldenrod, Physostegia, Heart Flow, Letting Go, Red Gladiolus, Letting Go, Crimean Snowdrop, Horse Chestnut Leaf Bud, True Power.

Physostegia

Physostegia virginiana ('Obedient Plant') & Amethyst

Indications: for integrity in interaction; for whenever we deny our integrity in our interactions with others; for when we find it hard to remain centred and connected; for when we respond inappropriately to situations because we have become un-centred or because we allow ourselves to be affected or influenced by what's going on around us; for when we allow our decisions to be swayed by external influences or by the ego dynamics of others; for whenever we feel overwhelmed or un-centred in work, study, or crisis situations; for conflict resolution: for the heart and solar plexus chakras.

❀

Physostegia helps us to become centred in the circle of ourselves – to stay in our integrity, so that we are able to peacefully observe whatever is going on around us, and can connect within to our intuition, to the truth of a situation, to how we are feeling and to what feels appropriate. In this way we can respond with detachment to situations without being pulled about by what's going on around us, or by other people's emotional or ego dynamics.

Physostegia encourages us to look at who, or what, we are obedient to – Who is our master? – Are we responding to life from the level of our ego-reactive, wounded child-self, or from the level of our Higher Self and the truth of a situation? Its Doctrine of Signatures reflects both the positive and negative aspects of these dynamics. Physostegia is a tall upright plant that grows in large clumps, with each stem standing strong and tall, on it's own within the clump. Arranged around the top of the stem are many rose-violet flowers. It is possible to push each flower from its original position to face in another direction. Once moved, the flower stays in its new position – hence the name 'Obedient Plant'. Physostegia encourages us to not allow ourselves to be pushed around by others or by what's going on around us.

If we find it hard to stand our ground and feel overwhelmed by those around us who have more forceful personalities, Physostegia inspires us to stay peacefully in our centre. It helps us to recognise what are our emotional dynamics, and what are other people's emotional and ego dynamics. It encourages us to leave other people's issues to them to deal with and it helps us to focus on what's going on for us, and what we need to do or to understand in a situation. Where there is bullying, Physostegia can be combined with Goldenrod, Orange Wallflower, Blue Delphinium, and either Red Poppy, or Inner Fire.

This essence can be used to bring greater integrity to group interaction. It can be added to a mist, for use in classroom or office situations, in order to reduce the level of reactivity between individuals, and to encourage centred, appropriate interaction (it is a key essence in the combination 'Self Worth', and is also in the combinations – 'Lighter Space', 'Working Harmony; and 'Light Heart Space' – see pages 178, 184 & 205).

Physostegia is the check-in, 'count to ten', and 'look before you leap' essence. It inspires us to get into the habit of pausing for long enough to become centred, before moving into action, so that we can connect with what's happening, and with what, (if anything), we need to do. If we're rushing about it helps us to check the order to do things in – to make sure that we haven't forgotten something, like our shopping list, or that phone call that we needed to make at a certain time. When we have a lot of complex tasks to do it helps us to see what it is that we need to do first, as well as anything else that we need to understand or to remember in order that we can be more effective in whatever we are doing. (In exam or complex work situations, combine Physostegia with Lilac and Speedwell – when writing about complex, multi-level subjects, add Blue Delphinium to this combination).

See also: Goldenrod, Speedwell, Lilac, Pussy Willow, Red Poppy, Blue Delphinium, Red Quince.

Pink Cherry

Prunus "Kanzan"

Indications: for whenever we have closed our heart to ourselves or to others; for when we are rigid or hard on ourselves or others; for anyone needing unconditional love and tenderness; for parents who find it hard to bond with a child; for children who need embracing and comforting; for the inner child; for those whose hearts are defended – who did not experience unconditional love as a child; for parents who do not know how to be gentle and loving towards their children because they themselves were not treated with unconditional love and gentleness in their own childhood; for those who deny themselves comfort and beauty in their lives: for the heart chakra.

Pink Cherry embodies the unconditional, tender love of a mother for a small child. This is the first gentle love that a mother gives her newborn child as she welcomes it into this world. Pink Cherry embodies the tenderness and softness, the comfort and security of the mother's arms – the warmth and nourishment from the mother, and the nourishing words of love that she softly speaks to the one she loves utterly and completely.

The archetypal unconditional mother says to the small child "I hear you, I see you, I feel you, I hold you and I understand how you feel. I will listen to you and support you. I am always there for you. You are totally lovable at all times, whatever you do, wherever you go."

Pink Cherry softens and opens our hearts to ourselves and to others. It teaches us how to be gentle and tender with ourselves and with others

– how to hold our inner child within our loving arms, and whisper to it tender words of unconditional love. It helps to gradually fill the aching void left from insufficient mothering, gently softening the defence that we may have built around our hearts during harsh times.

If, as very small children, we were not loved, or if we grew up in harsh environments in which how we felt was not acknowledged, or was judged as being 'soft' or a sign of weakness, we may now react by keeping our feelings and our sensitivity behind a protective shield, hiding how we feel from the world, out of fear of ridicule or rejection, even burying or hiding our feelings from ourselves. In this way we defend our hearts and become cut off from our own feelings and sensitivity. We may become stiff and judgemental towards ourselves as well towards those around us.

Pink Cherry helps to soften any hard-heartedness that we may have developed towards ourselves, or towards others. It gently opens the heart, encouraging us to allow more love and tenderness into our lives – to be kinder, more understanding and more compassionate towards ourselves and towards others. Those who benefit from this essence often cannot understand feelings and are afraid to explore them because of their inherited judgement about vulnerability and feelings.

This essence encourages us to allow more softness and femininity into our lives – more comfort, beauty and warmth – softer textured clothes, flowers, nice perfume, comfortable armchairs, soft rugs, soft cushions etc. When caring for babies, or the frail, it inspires gentleness and sensitivity, and when combined with essences such as Red Gladiolus, Horse Chestnut Leaf Bud, Pure Love and Yellow Hyacinth and Speedwell, it can bring sensitivity and gentleness to lovemaking.

Pink Cherry, when combined with Blue Delphinium enables us speak with greater understanding and sensitivity; when combined with Cyclamen, Pussy Willow and Grandmothers Arms, it encourages us to be kinder to ourselves and to lovingly nurture our physical, emotional, mental and spiritual needs.

See also: Cyclamen, Wild Cyclamen, Heart Mother, Orange Wallflower, Grandmothers Arms, Loving Me, Loving You.

Pure Love

Narcissus 'Paper White'

"Love one another but make not a bond of love;
Let it rather be a moving sea between the shores of your souls,
...Give your hearts, but not into each other's keeping.
For only the hand of life can contain your hearts.
And stand together, yet not too near together:
For the pillars of the temple stand apart.
And the oak tree and the cypress grow not in each other's shade"

– The Prophet – Kahil Gibran

Indications: for co-dependency and neediness in relationships; for when we yearn to be loved and to be in love; for loneliness; for the heart, brow and crown chakras.

❋

For purifying and clarifying the intentions of the heart and for understanding clearly the motivation and desires which influence our relationships. For clearing old patterns of co-dependency and the desire to have someone mirror our beauty and depth and light back to us. For letting go illusion around the narcissistic aspects of 'falling in love'. Pure Love helps us to see that when 'falling in love', we are, in fact, focusing on our own needs and our own sense of being lacking in love, rather than on true love.

When we are dreaming about creating an intimate relationship with someone – Pure Love helps us to not hold any illusions about the reality of what we are contemplating, or our motives. It helps to heal and clear the needy level of the ego from our heart, arising from childhood or past life wounding, and from lifetimes of human misperceptions about the true nature of love.

Because we have not recognised that we are always 'in love', and that that is our true essence, we have created unhealthy, needy bonds within our intimate, familial and social relationships. Fearing loss of love or approval we have maintained these co-dependent ties, by avoiding conflict and by denying our integrity and the truth of who we are and what is right and true for each of us. Pure Love helps us to realize that there is no lack of love, and to see and understand with love, where our own and other people's heart wounds lie. It encourages us to let go of old pain and illusion, to cut our co-dependent ties with others, and to open our heart to the infinite presence of love, which is the essence of our being, and the essence of all life.

As we clear these levels of pain and illusion from our hearts, we become more able to develop relationships that are independent, honest partnerships, in which, secure in our own love, we can honour our own and others' integrity, free from fear of loss of love or loss of approval, and free from unrealistic cultural expectations surrounding relationships. In so doing, we become independent in love and come to know and live a purer level of love. In place of neediness and desiring to be loved, we learn how to give love and how to be Love, and be 'in love' every moment of our day.

See also: Beauty in the Eye, With Love, Red Deadnettle, Orange Wallflower, Heart Flow, At the Heart of Being, Father Sun, Honesty, Blue Delphinium.

Pussy Willow

Salix daphnoides

Indications: for rigidity, inflexibility, resentment, exhaustion; not honouring our integrity; too much doing and never being; for when we have created difficult, pressured, stressful situations and rigid lifestyles; for tension, overwork and denial of our inner needs; for lack of connection to intuition; for lack of creativity; for when we don't allow comfort, relaxation, beauty, abundance or joy into our lives; for all chakras.

❄

The Doctrine of Signatures of Pussy Willow gives us a clue to its healing inspiration. All willows have an affinity to water, liking to grow in moist wet places. If a willow plant or tree remains connected to water it grows abundantly and remains healthy and flexible. If we cut a piece of willow and stick it in damp ground – so long as it has enough moisture, it will root and create a new and vigorous plant. Water is the element of connection to intuition, to the feminine and to the moon. Pussy Willow essence connects us to a more intuitive, flexible, flowing, right-brained approach to living.

The pussies, with their velvet silver softness take us back to childhood, to comfort, gentleness and caring. Pussy Willow essence connects us to our inner child and to our need for life to be comfortable, flowing, gentle, caring and unstressed. The pussies also reflect the silver of the moon and the moon's effects on the tides of our life, and our need to go with the flow of our inner rhythms, and the rhythms and true timing of the flow of life as it unfolds and develops.

Basket willow plants are cut back to a stump or stool every winter and rapidly grow a mass of long straight stems over the coming year, ready for next winter's cropping. This reflects willow's connection to abundance and creativity, mirroring to us the abundance and creativity that we manifest whenever we are connected through our intuition and our connection to the flow of life – to what is truly comfortable and appropriate.

Willows retain their flexibility so long as they remain connected to water. If the weather becomes hot and they cannot draw on life-giving water then a willow will begin to crack and split. Large trees will suddenly lose whole limbs, which will crack and split off from the main trunk. If we burn willow on an open fire it cracks and spits red sparks and glowing embers across the room. Similarly if we have too much fire in our lives, too much action, and are driving ourselves too hard in a left-brained linear timetabled fashion, we soon become rigid and resentful and crack and spit at those around us, or at life, and may eventually crack in some way, or have an accident or become ill.

The left-brain sees things in a linear way It likes structure, timetabling and routine, is logical and concerned with structural ideas, regimented routines, and a 'right' or 'wrong' way of doing things. The left-brain is useful and we need it to function in this dimension. However, we function much better if we balance our left-brain skills with those of our right brain, in order to ground, manifest and structure our creativity and ideas. We need to integrate both, for the marriage of structure and practicality, with the more lateral qualities of creativity, intuition, flexibility and connection to true timing.

Until recently in the west our society was largely driven by left-brained, linear, structured ways of thinking and working. These approaches have created a high level of work and lifestyle related stress and dis-ease, as a result of being too inflexible and too unrelated to the reality of human life and to how we as humans function best. There is now a movement towards trying to create a better balance by combining both linear and lateral approaches to the creation and management of organisations and social structures, in the hope that they may become more human and flexible, more integrated and co-operative, more responsive to change and open to new ideas and inspiration; as well as more creative, holistic, caring and compassionate.

Pussy Willow inspires us to go with the real flow of life and events – to follow what is truly comfortable and appropriate – to respond to our inner rhythms and to our real sense of timing. It inspires us to know that life supports us, if we support and honour ourselves on a daily basis, and it encourages us to listen to our intuition – our gut feeling – to what feels truly comfortable at any time. Our intuition will always talk to us about what is real – what feels right, even when our left-brain may be arguing and saying that our intuition is irrational and unreasonable. If we follow what feels right, despite the 'rational' arguments of our head, we will frequently find out after the event just why our intuition was correct.

Pussy Willow helps us when we are trying to find new ways of being that will bring healing to our lives, to how we work, and to how we organise our work and our days. It encourages us to trust that we can live a life that is loving, healing, comfortable, creative, abundant and enjoyable, and it inspires us to realise that our life will begin to work in magical and unforeseen ways once we open ourselves to a more expansive, flexible, connection to life and to untold new, possibilities. Pussy Willow helps us to realise that nothing is denied us – that we only deny ourselves.

See also: Speedwell, Cyclamen, Living the Dream, Heart Mother, Lilac, With Love, Disciple of the Heart and Physostegia.

Red Clover

Trifolium pratense

Indications: panic, terror, fear, worry, for when we worry about what 'might' happen; for when we hook into fearful thought forms related to world events, or to disease, pollution, food scares, fear of attack; or fear for the safety and health of friends and loved ones; for fear of abandonment 'in extremis'; fear of death and dying; for the fearful child in our psyche; for when we are anxious or afraid but don't know why.

❉

Red Clover relates to the archetypal father energy embodied by such mythic figures as Santa Claus/Father Christmas – the deep, hearty, comforting presence that warmly reassures the frightened child within the human psyche, embodying peace and safety and the message that all is well. Red Clover says to us with great compassion and a rich belly laugh – " Don't Panic! Settle Down. Relax. All is Well". It encourages us to settle into our peace in the moment, to get things in perspective – to stop worrying or getting into a state about what 'might' happen. It teaches us how to create an experience of peace and safety; how to reassure our frightened child, and how to help it to feel safe and supported, whatever situation we are in.

Most of us, at one time or another, have met firemen or paramedics whose very presence reassures and supports those around them – whose warmth, humour and peaceful, unhurried actions create an atmosphere of safety around them. This essence helps us to create just such an atmosphere of peace and safety for ourselves and for others. It shows us how our fearful thoughts are just fearful thoughts, and it encourages us to settle down into our peace, and to stop panicking.

Red Clover shows us just how powerful our thoughts are, and how our thinking affects our experience, and the energy that we resonate into the world. It reminds us that we do have a choice about what we fill our minds with, particularly in relation to fearful information and stories portrayed in the media.

By staying in our peace, we encourage an atmosphere of peace around us, and a resonance of peace in the world. The more we can all manage to do this in our daily lives, the more an atmosphere of peace, safety, trust and positive goodwill will arise in the world. The fewer people that buy into the illusion of fear, the more we will come to know peace on earth.

Red Clover is grounding, settling, comforting and warming – particularly for the base, sacral, solar plexus and heart chakas. It brings a strong sense of being supported, of not being alone, and of being deeply partnered and supported by spirit every moment of our life. It encourages us to not take life too seriously, and it teaches us how to laugh a rich deep belly laugh at the illusion of fear.

Red Clover shows us that whatever happens we are safe, and that even in death, we are held in the loving arms of our infinite self and our spiritual friends and guardians. It reminds us that we are not powerless mortals, but are instead infinite, creative, divine beings.

At this time we have the possibility of walking away from aeons of 'mortal' fear that we have created and maintained since the time we first began to separate in our perceptions from the experience of our divine being. Red Clover is one of those essences that can inspire us at this time, to experience the reality and peace of our divine being here on earth – to know the peace of heaven on earth.

See also: Divine Being, Stitchwort, Letting Go, Peaceful Detachment, Living the Dream, Crimean Snowdrop, Cherry Plum Fruit, Sky Blue Comfrey.

Red Deadnettle

Lamium purpureum and clear quartz

Indications: for the pain of rejection; for broken-heartedness, deep anger, bitterness, and the loneliness of feeling rejected; for old pain of rejection from childhood or other lives; for loss of confidence and loss of self-worth following rejection; for when we project our fear of being rejected on to others, in expectation of rejection; for the heart and solar plexus chakras.

Red Deadnettle addresses our yearning to be loved, and the pain, anger, bitterness and loneliness that arises, when we feel that we have been rejected. It inspires us to realise that we only experience loss of love, when we close our hearts to ourselves and to others, out of pain and judgement and fear. Red Deadnettle re-opens our hearts to ourselves, and to the ever-present love within and around us, with which we can fill our whole being, at any time.

It helps us to embrace the rejected child within our hearts and it shows us how we may connect to others, with a full and free heart beyond the level of our wounded child self. It encourages us to let go of the expectations and demands for love and friendship that we place on others, and teaches us instead, to give to ourselves the love, support and approval that we have sought from others. In this way we learn to become independent and free in our relationships, no longer co-dependant out of fear of loss of love, and no longer needing or demanding love from others as a 'right'.

When we defend our hearts, fearing rejection, others around us pick up on our insecurity and the pressure of our neediness. Feeling the intensity of our expectations, they may begin to pull away, and the very thing that we dread happening comes to pass – we find ourselves rejected. Red Deadnettle shows us, that as long as we believe that love comes from outside ourselves and can be taken away from us, all our relationships will be co-dependent to some extent. We will always be afraid of love being withheld and will modify our actions and sacrifice our honesty and integrity in order to continue to be loved by another.

Red Deadnettle takes the sting out of rejection by handing us the key to our hearts and to infinite love. It shows us that there is a wellspring of infinite love arising within our hearts. From this eternal wellspring, we can flood our whole being with love at any time, and allow that love to flow freely from us, knowing that this love is limitless and that it is always available to us all. Love can never be withheld, it is only us, in our judgment of ourselves, who cut ourselves off from the infinite source of our love that lies within us.

Red Deadnettle shows us how the world mirrors back to us our beliefs about life. We come to realise that the more that we embrace love and the more that we love ourselves and others, the more we will find love reflected back to us in all that we experience.

As we begin to love ourselves, and learn to fill our own pot, it becomes easier for us to relate to others with honesty and independence. We begin to discover what true love is, and we learn to give freely and unconditionally, without expectations, and without sacrificing our integrity.

Sometimes we have to be prepared "to lose all to gain all", when relating to others – to be brave enough to honour ourselves and to be honest and true at all times, even if this creates the possibility that the other person may reject us. Ultimately a relationship is only wholesome and sustainable to the degree in which each person honours themselves, and is honest and true to themselves and to their partners. In reality we have nothing to lose, but it can sometimes feel that way as we take our first steps towards independence and honesty in our relationships.

See also: Phoenix Rebirth, Heart Flow, Pure Love, Physostegia, Blue Delphinium, Goldenrod, Heart Mother, Red Quince and Inner Fire.

Red Gladiolus

Gladiolus sp.

Indications: for when we need to look at our original motivation and choice to enter into a sexual relationship with a particular person, and our reasons for consenting to make love at any given time; for women who have experienced a split between the spiritual expression of love and sexuality, and their actual physical and emotional experience (often in response to abuse or sexual acts devoid of love and sensitivity); for men who wish to have a greater understanding of women's sexuality and sensitivity; for women who feel 'turned off' sex in some way, either because there is some degree of aversion or distaste arising from past experiences, or because of feeling under too much emotional or psychological pressure, to satisfy another's need.

Red Gladiolus inspires us to look at how true we have been to ourselves and to others in our sexual relationships. It also asks us to consider, and to understand without judgement, what our original motivation and intention is, in choosing to enter into a sexual relationship with another – and at whether we honour our integrity, express our truth and acknowledge to ourselves and to our partner, the reason why we consent to 'make love' on any given occasion.

Red Gladiolus asks us to look at whether we feel able to honestly show our true self to another, and to speak openly to our partner about our sexuality, our feelings and our preferences. It also addresses how much we love our body, or our partner's body, and enjoy and celebrate our sexuality. It asks whether we hold back from sharing deep intimacy and profound soul connection with our partner, because of judgements we hold against them or against ourselves. Are we afraid to say no – afraid of abuse? Are we inhibited out of a fear of being judged to be inadequate in some way, a fear of pregnancy, a fear of sexually transmitted disease, in reaction to past unloving experiences, or because we do not find our partner attractive?

Men and women share a long history, co-created around the experience of sexuality. We each carry different aspects of the story – from memories of sublime, divine union – to memories of violent abuse and rape. Although sexuality is no longer as hidden as it was – there is still a lot of prudishness, awkwardness and lack of down to earth normality and open-ness around sexuality. Media portrayal, cultural or religious prudishness, playground dirty jokes, crude pornography, prejudice about homosexuality and lesbianism, lack of open, relaxed discussion about sexuality and sexual relationships – may all have influenced how we feel about sex, and may have contributed to any feelings we now have of inhibition or distaste.

Two of the key areas we are addressing at this time within relationships, are communication and co-dependency. When we feel less than whole in ourselves and seek love, approval or recognition from another, we may try to modify our behaviour or the way we look, in order to gain love or approval, often to the extent of being afraid to speak our truth or to honour what feels right for us. In some ways this is true for most of our relationships at this time. Added to this we may feel inhibited about discussing with our partner, the sexual side of our relationship, since sexuality is still a subject about which many feel un-relaxed about discussing, and one which can raise painful, mixed emotions, with the possibility of either person feeling judged or rejected by the other.

The shift towards transparency and equality of worth at this time is affecting all areas of our experience including our sexuality and sexual relationships. Now, soul to soul, heart to heart, mind to mind, body to body, men and women together, women and women together and men and men together, we have the opportunity to express our truth, and to share deeply our love, without fear, without dominion, in powerful union.

Red Gladiolus also relates to women's sexuality and to women's need to experience love and deep connection within their experience of physical sexuality. Often a split occurs for women, between the spiritual and emotional expression of love and sexuality, and their actual physical experience. This may have arisen out of past sexual experiences in which they felt unable to express integrity and love within the physical experience of sex: experiences of sexual trauma, abuse, or sexual acts devoid of love or sensitivity, or in response to family, cultural, religious, media or peer group images of female and male sexuality. There may be feelings of inner repulsion, distaste and inhibition in relation to sex, or inner conflict and confusion resulting in periods of either promiscuity or avoidance of sex.

Red Gladiolus encourages women to love and honour their sexuality, and to come to a place of honesty and integrity about the choices they make within and about, their sexual relationships, so that ultimately 'lovemaking' becomes the wholehearted, undefended, joyful expression of love, freely and lovingly given, without judgement, inhibition or coercion.

The inspiration of Red Gladiolus may also be used by men, to bring a greater understanding and awareness of female sexuality and sensitivity.

When healing from experiences of sexual abuse, we often need to go through a forgiveness process – a letting go of judgment of ourselves and of others – a return to innocence. Forgiveness processes, such as The Campfire Process (as outlined in Brandon Bays book 'The Journey') can profoundly transform and heal our experience of ourselves and of others. There is also a need to embrace our anger, to set boundaries, and to honour what is right for us at any given time. In this way we move away from being a 'victim', to a co-creator, and can begin to heal our experience with understanding and integrity. The inspiration of many of the essences listed below can be called on to help us in this process.

See also: Blue Delphinium, Horse Chestnut Leaf Bud, Pure Love, Heart Flow, Loving Me, Loving You, Beauty in the Eye, Yellow Hyacinth, Phoenix Rebirth, Original Innocence, Physostegia, Red Deadnettle, Letting Go, Honesty, Crab Apple Fruit, Father Sun, Child's Play.

Red Poppy

Papaver rhoeas

Indications: for issues around anger and powerlessness; for whenever we feel 'stuck' or trapped by a situation; for when we are afraid to set boundaries or to say no; for swings between angry outbursts and suppression of anger; for repeated unconstructive anger; for resignation, powerlessness and feeling a victim of circumstance; for depression, resentment; frustration, resignation; for when we get angry, then crumple into hopelessness and guilt; for when we allow ourselves to be abused; for timidity, passivity and patterns of low vitality, stagnation or frustration of energy and lack of motivation or drive.

Red Poppy looks at anger and at how we use our fire and motivating energy throughout our lives. It addresses how positively we deal with situations that need changing in our lives. Red Poppy encourages us to keep the fire energy moving and flowing in our lives, so that we do not end up in situations where we feel powerless and frustrated, where our anger and frustrated fire energy turns in on itself and stagnates, or explodes uncontrollably.

Red Poppy embraces a whole range of anger issues. It asks us to look at whether we are using our anger to bring about constructive change, or whether we are either suppressing it through fear – or are resorting to frequent unproductive angry outbursts that merely serve as a way of venting our frustration and desperation, and do nothing to actually change the situation that we find ourselves in.

When we repeatedly feel unable to bring about positive change in our lives, in relation to situations that are no longer healthy or tolerable, we begin to lose confidence. We become resentful, angry, depressed, and often see ourselves as a victim. Whenever we find ourselves saying "I can't" Red Poppy helps us to turn that into an "I can" state of mind, encouraging us to take charge of our life and our destiny, to peacefully and assertively set boundaries, and to take positive steps to bring about any change that is needed in our circumstances. It helps us to get positive movement and energy flowing in our life so that we can channel suppressed or frustrated anger into creating a constructive way forward for all.

Red Poppy helps us to realise that there is a reason why we get angry and it encourages us to look at what that reason is, and what we need to do in order to change our situation, and to not get caught in repeated cycles of unresolved issues in our life. Where there is fear of anger and fear of speaking out, the inspiration of Red Poppy can be used together with that of Blue Delphinium, Cherry Plum Fruit, Physostegia, Honesty and Goldenrod.

Red Poppy has a steady fire energy and can be taken over a long period of time to help us to rebuild our confidence, and to enable us to move out of patterns of powerlessness, suppression of anger, negativity, victim mentality, and unconstructive use of anger.

There are times when we need to bring an end to a difficult situation, and have to muster a large amount of clarity and fire energy in order for our action to be powerful, decisive and effective (particularly if we are not a very fiery type of person) – in this case we may find it helpful to use Inner Fire for a week to ten days in order to support us in meeting this challenge. (Inner Fire should not generally be used for more than ten days at a time, without a break of several weeks.)

See also: Blue Delphinium, Cherry Plum Fruit, Physostegia, Goldenrod, Honesty, Father Sun, Inner Fire, Heart Flow, Phoenix Rebirth, Loving Me, Loving You, Blue Salvia, Red Quince, Red Deadnettle, True Power, Passionate Life, Living the Dream.

Red Quince

Chaenomeles speciosa "Simonii"

*"Have you learned lessons only of those who admired you,
and were tender with you, and stood aside for you?*

*Have you not learned great lessons from those who braced
themselves against you, and disputed the passage with you?"*

- Walt Whitman – "Leaves of Grass"

Indications: hypersensitivity to judgement; taking everything personally; painful defensiveness; aggressive defensive reaction against hearing the truth about oneself (arising out of the pain of low self-worth and self-hatred); feeling 'got at', misunderstood, and a victim in life; for when we close our heart and ears in pain; for when we wrongly interpret what someone says, taking it as a judgement against ourselves; for bitterness and cynicism.

Red Quince is for when we take everything personally, reacting out of old, buried pain and lack of self-esteem. We move into patterns of defensive aggressive behaviour, and feeling 'got at', when our self worth is low, and when the situation we are in reminds us of past painful experiences in which we felt that love or approval was withdrawn from us. When others try to communicate with us, we are so caught in our pain, that we do not feel 'big enough' to be able to listen with detachment to discern what is or isn't true in what they are saying. Often we mis-hear what they are saying, interpreting it as a judgement against us, when this is not necessarily the case.

Our reactivity arises from past experiences in which we have encountered judgement and the withdrawal of love. When we encounter similar experiences, our wounded child/self tries to block the possibility of hearing any more judgement, or feeling any more pain. Out of fear of loss of love, and out of a sense of guilt, self-judgement and self-hatred, we close our hearts and ears, not only to others but also to ourselves.

Red Quince helps us to enfold our wounded child/self with unconditional love, to begin to heal the childhood wounds of judgement and loss. This allows our inner child to relax, to regain its innocence and confidence, and to open its heart once again to love and truth. Drawing on the inspiration of Red Quince we learn how to unconditionally love and support ourselves. In this way we no longer feel so threatened by life, or by what others might have to say. We can listen with an open, detached heart and mind, for what is true or not, without engaging in ego confrontation (the confrontation of wounded child/selves) and without feeling 'got at' or a victim.

As, we become 'big enough' to embrace the truth about ourselves, and are more able to hear and see the truth in what others say, and in our life experiences, we learn not to judge ourselves so harshly if we feel that we have made a 'mistake'. Red Quince encourages us to grasp the opportunity to learn from our experiences, and to grow as a result of them, without feeling as though we can never hold our head up again. It takes the 'sting' out of judgement, and helps us to we accept the truth lightly, with compassion and self-worth, so that when we do have something to learn, or behaviour to change, we no longer feel crushed by self-judgment or by the judgment of others

With the maturity we gain from integrating Red Quince's teaching, we become grateful for life's lessons and for those who reveal the truth to us about ourselves. We learn to listen peacefully without reaction, and with curiosity, to see what is true, and what it is that we might need to embrace. Red Quince also helps us to not buy into other people's emotional ego agendas, but to listen impartially for truth, without judgement of their issues, whilst still honouring our own heart and integrity.

See also: Physostegia, Yellow Hyacinth, Pink Cherry, Goldenrod, Honesty, Blue Delphinium, Original Innocence, Grandmothers Arms, Phoenix Rebirth, Red Deadnettle, Red Poppy, Peaceful Detachment, True Power

Reunion

Fraxinus excelsior

Indications: for whenever there is a lack of integration of awareness, a lack of balance, or an experience of separation or split; for those whose framework of reference is largely lateral, literal and two dimensional, who experience difficulty integrating multi-level awareness and multi sensory awareness; also for those whose vision is predominantly right-brained and multi dimensional, and who lack focus and grounding; for whenever we feel unable to integrate or to sustain multi-dimensional awareness.

Reunion assists with the integration and deep synthesis of multi-dimensional awareness and the many levels of being – of left and right brain; masculine and feminine; within and without; seen and unseen; spirit and matter. It inspires our understanding of the union of polar opposites within the whole – duality and one-ness within one being – the grounding of the divine, and the divinity of matter.

Reunion relates to whenever we are divided, internally conflicted in some way, or seeking to integrate and balance various aspects of our being. It can be used by anyone who has experienced separation from a twin, or a split from some aspect of their being. It can also be used when two people, or two parties, are pulling in opposite directions and need to work together. Reunion helps both parties to integrate harmoniously, so that their individual qualities and contributions can be combined to create a successful and balanced partnership.

This essence can be used whenever we experience life from either a predominantly right-brained, or a predominantly left-brained viewpoint, and for when we have difficulty integrating both linear and lateral perspectives. Reunion helps us to develop a more integrated and balanced vision of life. It may be taken continually over a long period of time to assist us in developing the capacity to integrate and draw on both linear and lateral awareness, and to integrate multi-level awareness as we move into multi-dimensionality at this time.

Reunion inspires us to find a still point of awareness and integration, and it can be used, together with other essences to come into a way of living meditation and attunement, throughout our day. It is the stillness (no-mind) within the movement of being that allows awareness and integration. (see "At One" meditation combination p.186). Reunion reminds us that true wisdom is all-knowing, and that to be all-knowing, is to know no-thing.

In astrological terms Reunion is an essence of Mercury, particularly of communication – both visible and invisible, spoken and unspoken – the communication that travels instantaneously and continuously, between and within all Being, along the light lines of the web that connects all being – the timeless, infinite, ever-changing movement and song of creation.

This essence was made from the twin ash tree that grows in our garden, which is the guardian tree for the surrounding landscape. At the height of three feet this tree divides into two trunks that rise up together. Each trunk then divides into two, appearing as if two people are standing together with arms upraised, but joined as one at the base.

A few years ago I had a profound experience with this ash tree in which I was momentarily thrown into multi-dimensional awareness and saw the tree and everything else in the world, stones, grass, insects, trees and people, in constant communication with each other. All communication flowed continuously, in a stream of intelligent light between each and everything. Overwhelmed by receiving so much information at one time, I shut down, feeling I hadn't the capacity to integrate such a multi-dimensional experience for more than a moment. Even though at the time I was unable to sustain this experience, it nonetheless completely changed my perception of the reality of the world around me, and eventually led to the creation of this essence, part of whose purpose is in helping us to develop the capacity to sustain and to integrate multi-dimensional experiences at this time.

In the Celtic Ogham, Nuin (Ash) links past, present and future – continual birth and re-birth. The keys symbolise universal understanding of how all things are linked and connected. In Norse mythology, Odin hung from Yggdrasil (the Ash tree) to gain the secrets of the runes and enlightenment. (source – 'The Sacred Tree' by Glennie Kindred)

See also: Rosebay Willowherb, One Being, At the Heart of Being, Lilac, Speedwell, Child's Play, Blue Delphinium.

Rosebay Willowherb

Epliobium angustifolium

Indications: fear of expanded awareness and fundamental shifts in perception; for when we feel disconnected from the natural world and the earth, and wish to connect to the spirit in nature.

❊

For welcoming and allowing increasing expansion of awareness of the multi-dimensional reality of all life; for transforming our fear of radical shifts in perception; for connection to the spirit in nature, to the natural world and to the earth; for grounding our awareness in our hearts, in the recognition of the divine in all; for deep appreciation of the beauty and countless gifts that we receive from the earth and from the natural world.

At this time of rapidly expanding consciousness, we find our perceptions changing daily as we move from the limited known 'security' of a three dimensional experience of life, into an expanded fourth dimensional awareness. At times this can seem unsettling, as all that previously represented security (even if it was limited or fear-bound), falls away, and we seek new ways to ground and integrate our awareness.

Through the essence of Rosebay Willowherb, the devic world beckons and offers us a safe route into multi-dimensional awareness It inspires us to recognise the conscious movement of light that forms the 'substance' of all 'physical' matter on Earth and of every cell in nature. Through this recognition we are able to ground our divine, spiritual awareness deeply into our experience of being here on this planet. By changing our perception of the 'physical' world, we anchor divine perception into the whole planet, and thus the earth responds, and together with the devas and spirits who join with us in at this time, we create 'heaven on earth'.

Rosebay Willowherb helps us to see and give thanks for the beauty and gifts of the earth and the natural world. It deepens our connection to nature, to the trees, rocks, plants and creatures – the herbs that heal, the animal spirits that guide us – and to the ways in which we can work together with the spirits of this place, to heal and care for the earth and for ourselves. It seems fitting that we have the gift of flower essences at this time, to deepen our connection to our own divine essence and to the divine essence in all life, on earth and elsewhere.

See also: Reunion, Sweet Pea, Grandmother's Arms, Heart Mother, Green Alexanders, Bluebell Grove and Stitchwort.

Sky Blue Comfrey

Symphytum aspermum (sky blue)

"Behold, I make all things new"

Indications: fear of mortality; fear of aging, and fear of loss of health, beauty and capabilities through aging; feelings of insecurity triggered by perceptions of aging and mortality; fear of separation through death.

❋

For infinite dynamic peace; divine peace; knowing that we are, and always have been infinite, that time and death are an illusion – that there is only now; that nothing and no-one are ever lost, and that nothing can harm us; for relaxing into the total peace and joy of divine being, into infinite safety and freedom from suffering.

Sky Blue Comfrey takes us into a realisation of timelessness – that time does not exist, except in our perceptions – that there is, and only ever has been, now – the moment that we are in. It shows us that each moment is new – that we can relax and expand deeply into the infinity of our being, within the timelessness of each moment. It inspires us to let go our perceptions of time and of the passage of time; of aging, and of all the illusory 'what ifs'; and to relax instead into the constantly new movement of infinite and joyful being.

Sky Blue Comfrey addresses our perceptions of death and mortality. It inspires us to realise that we are invulnerable and infinite – that we never lose anything or anyone through death – and that we no longer need to re-create experiences of struggle and suffering through fear, but can allow ourselves now to settle deeply into the joy of timeless being.

We know from the work of Deepak Chopra, and many others, that our continuing youthfulness is greatly influenced by the degree in which we choose to live our lives fully and richly in the moment, – and that the aging process is often triggered and accelerated by our perception that aging is an 'inevitable', time-determined fact. We have also come to realise that our healing and regeneration processes are supported by our belief in our ability to heal, and by our joy in living life to the full – physically, emotionally, mentally and spiritually – rather than by our fear of mortality. Sky Blue Comfrey supports us in this realisation.

See also: Original Innocence, Crab Apple Fruit, White Yarrow, Stitchwort, Comfrey, Letting Go, Sweet Hunza, Sweet Pea, Divine Being, Speedwell, Bluebell Grove, Green Alexanders.

Speedwell

Veronica persica

Indications: For when we try to go too fast, rushing ahead without connecting to the present moment; for overactive, tense, speedy states; for distraction, lack of focus or attention, making mistakes; for when we are accident prone or clumsy; for whenever we feel that we do not have enough time; for when we drive ourselves in order to meet deadlines; for when our mind races or frets over problems; for when we don't take the time we need; for when we live in our heads, ahead of ourselves, dreaming of future ideas and schemes; for fear of connection – fear of being fully present.

For dynamic, centred stillness – being fully present and connected in the moment, seeing true; for relaxed, alert concentration and attention to detail; for meditation and connection to intuition and guidance; for coming into timelessness.

Speedwell teaches us how to take our time – how to take time to connect and time to think – time to be – time to look at what's in front of us and really see – time to listen – time to really enjoy doing something – time to relax – time to do something really well. It says that there is all the time in the world, and it takes us into an experience of the deep infinity of time – a wonderful expansion of timelessness. In this infinite timeless space we settle deeply into a rich expanse of now in which there is always time for what we have to do.

Speedwell can profoundly change our experience of time. When we let go our feeling that there isn't enough time, extraordinary things

142

happen in the shortest enriched moments of being. Things that we thought would be 'hard work' and would take forever, are somehow accomplished in the most wonderful and easy fashion. Speedwell reminds us that there is only now. Life becomes a living meditation – a rich experience of peace in the moment. Our focus and attention are fully present in the moment. In this timeless immersion and deep connection, our mind settles into an infinitely expanded and relaxed receptivity, and we become able to draw on wonderful inspiration and understanding. This is not a process of hard work, but is instead a deep allowing of information to flow gently into one's conscious mind.

This essence helps us to trust that all good things will come together beautifully in time. Through the magical inspiration of Speedwell we begin to really enjoy our journey – to have the 'time of our life', right now, rather than our mind being focussed on some future goal or experience. Each now moment becomes a rich source of creativity, inspiration and learning. By connecting to the now, we can connect and respond to whatever is most appropriate in the moment, and to where our focus needs to be. In this way things happen at the 'right' time, and in the 'right' way, easily and enjoyably.

Speedwell frees us up. Our soul has longed for deep connection, and for the peace of timelessness. Freed from a belief in limited time, we re-enter the realm of divine being and the realisation that time does not exist. In timelessness all things become possible and everything is accessible. As we re-connect with our timeless being – the one in all that we are and always have been, we draw on our accumulated wisdom, skills, and understanding.

Part of the dynamic of this time of clearing and transformation is the experience of time speeding up. At the same time, for many people there is that sense that one has only just dealt with one challenging situation or issue, and immediately there is something else to deal with. There are also those whose job or life situation are like that all the time – mothers with several young children, nurses and doctors in accident and emergency wards.

Whenever we find ourselves becoming stressed by the pace of events in our lives, or by the fast energy of this time, Speedwell can help us to come into our still point. The image I have is of a vortex swirling rapidly. The only still place is in the centre, where we are unaffected by all the rush and turmoil around us – and where we can experience the bliss of peace. Perhaps this is the purpose of this sense of things speeding up. The faster things feel, the more we are forced into our centre, as we come to realise that this is the only place where we will find peace and will survive the pace.

Apart from our perception of lack of time, and therefore our constant rushing to 'be in time', there are other reasons why we do not connect and pay attention in the moment. Often we have a deep fear of connection. For some it can be because of hyper-sensitivity and a fear of one's senses being flooded and overwhelmed with information. For others there may be a fear of the vastness of multi-dimensional awareness, and of who we may be, or an inability to block out other people's emotional energy. Where there is sensitivity to other people's emotional energy, Speedwell can be combined with Peaceful Detachment. Where there is a fear of expanded awareness, combine Speedwell with Reunion. In study environments, combine Speedwell with Lilac, Reunion and Disciple of the Heart.

Some children, who have experienced or witnessed traumatic or abusive situations, may be very wary of connecting with others or with life, not wanting to open themselves up again to pain, shock or trauma. Sometimes this fear is masked by hyperactivity, poor attention span and inappropriate, disconnected behaviour. For these children, Speedwell may be used regularly, over a prolonged period of time, together with Crimean Snowdrop, Cherry Plum Fruit, Original Innocence, Phoenix Rebirth and Reunion. Cranio-sacral therapy, particularly when given by an experienced practitioner over a period of several months, can help these children to gradually relax and feel safe enough to slow down, and to re-connect with themselves and with life.

See also: Sky Blue Comfrey, Comfrey, Blue Salvia, Lilac, Pussy Willow, Living the Dream, Bluebell Grove, With Love, Cyclamen, Crab Apple Fruit, The Rose, Divine Being, Passionate Life, Disciple of the Heart, Grandmothers Arms, One Being, At the Heart of Being, Child's Play, Golden Blessings.

Stitchwort

Stellaria holostea

Indications: Fear of fully incarnating and fully living, limiting fears of suffering and 'physical' mortality; feelings of acute vulnerability and sensitivity; having cold feet in relation to living; for the crown, solar plexus, sacral and base chakras.

For commitment to full embodiment as a divine being here on earth, at this time; for grounding the light of divine perception and experience into all 'physical' matter and life experience; for settling down into the safety of our essential invulnerable and infinite being; for moving beyond the illusion of separation and mortality.

Stitchwort essence is for those who find it hard to commit themselves to being fully here, on this planet at this time – particularly those, who as a result of past experiences, are afraid of illness, suffering and mortality. They may be highly sensitive and may not feel robust enough to cope with the hustle and bustle of life on earth without the security of strong support from others.

Those who benefit from this essence often appear fragile, may frequently be ill, exhausted, pale or cold, and emotionally or psychically porous. Some yearn for other, less dense worlds. Often, because of fear, these souls find it hard to stay fully present in their bodies – all of their energetic movement is upwards, in an attempt to avoid engaging in a world they find so frightening.

In many ways Stitchwort addresses the frightened child within each of us, and many of the illusory deep fears that have developed in the human psyche since the time of separation. Sometimes these fears have arisen out of experiences in which we have tried to 'jump out' in terror – sometimes from past traumatic experiences in which we have literally 'jumped out' of our body, or 'jumped off' the planet.

Stitchwort is one of those essences that re-affirm to us that we experience fear and suffering and pain when we resist and pull away from what is happening and from the experience of infinite peace, which lies at the invulnerable core of our being. The pain and terror comes from pulling so far away from our centre, our peace – our home. One of our greatest incarnation opportunities at this time is to move beyond the illusion of separation and mortality.

Stitchwort encourages us to change the way that we view the world, to re-affirm our purpose and choice to be here at this time, to recognise that this is not a 'physical' world, but a constantly changing multi-dimensional world, reflecting the movement of spirit and consciousness. " My father's house has many mansions", and this planet is just another aspect of the divine, albeit often unrecognised.

Therein lies our purpose at this time – to recognise and experience our own divinity and invulnerability – to see and be in communion with the divine in all, and to settle down and feel safe in this world, knowing that it is as divine and safe a place to be as anywhere else in heaven. Stitchwort also shows us that we are all interconnected beings, that we are not alone, and that we will always get the help and support that we need when we need it. This encourages us to relax and to settle down and become more adventurous in our exploration of life.

Stitchwort also addresses those pioneering souls whose incarnation role at this time is to anchor the light of divine consciousness here on earth. These are the ice-breakers who go ahead of others in the awakening journey of consciousness on this planet – whose challenge is to awaken their own memory of divine consciousness here on earth and thereby awaken the memory of the divine in the consciousness of others and of the earth itself.

Sensing the depth and density of the energies they will need to transform through their own human experience, these souls often balk at their chosen role and become afraid of how far into darkened areas of consciousness they will need to travel in order to rekindle the light of divine being. Often they feel an aching sense of loneliness on their journey, unable to communicate to others the profundity of their experience – sometimes grieving and yearning for close communion with their soul group.

Stitchwort brings peace and courage to these souls, enabling them to draw on the light of the divine, by connecting to their own divine being and to the divine consciousness in the cosmos and here on earth – until they become like a radar star on earth, receiving and transmitting divine light into all areas of consciousness and awareness.

Stitchwort inspires us to enjoy being fully here in our body, on the earth, and to enjoy physical activity and connection to the natural world and the earth. Any activity that builds physical confidence and helps us to connect to our body and to being on the earth, will support the healing inspiration of Stitchwort: – swimming, walking (especially in a natural place, or park), running, cycling, canoeing, Tai Chi, gardening, planting trees, eating good wholesome food, cooking, good sex, dance, playing with children, caring for animals, studying biology, making flower essences, studying and using herbs, enjoying the beauty and miracle of the world – the company of friends, hot water in the shower, the wind on your face.

Other supportive measures which help to integrate the inspiration of Stitchwort are: – breathing gently and deep into the lower abdomen and then down into one's legs and feet; becoming aware of, and dropping any tension in the abdominal area and the shoulders; taking gradually increasing steps towards standing on one's own two feet, becoming more independent, spending more time alone, setting healthy boundaries and becoming more adventurous on one's own.

The Doctrine of Signatures of Stitchwort reflects its indications. It is a delicate, fresh green, tall, thin-stemmed plant, which grows in masses on grassy banks. Each stem is flimsy and topped by small, star-like white flowers in May. All the stems grow up together and support each other, as well as being supported by the surrounding grass. The whole plant and the flowers constantly reach upwards to the light. If you follow each stem to the ground, you will find that it is not directly rooted into the ground, but is joined instead to a runner that lies above the ground, and to which all the stems in the group are attached. This runner then puts down very tentative roots into the soil, at intervals along it's length.

Interestingly, when I re-made this essence this year, I went to several clumps of Stitchwort growing en masse in the shelter of a tall hedge but was led away from them until finally, after visiting many patches of Stitchwort I came to a few pioneering solitary plants growing out in the open, on the edge of a trout lake. This is unusual for Stitichwort which always prefers growing with the support of a whole clump of plants. In order to make this essence I was drawn to take a single plant stem, from a plant growing strongly alone. It was connected to the other plants by the usual over-ground runner system, but was happy to grow alone in the open beside deep water. Somehow this felt significant in relation to the teaching of this essence.

Since, by nature, the souls who respond to Stitchwort often have a more feminine/yin/watery receptive nature, it may be helpful to combine Stitchwort with more earth and fire essences such as Father Sun, Red Poppy, Inner Fire, Green Alexanders, Heart Mother, Passionate Life, Physostegia, Goldenrod, At the Heart of Being, Child's Play, Wild Cyclamen, Red Gladiolus etc., as well as with other essences that address fear – such as: Divine Being, Letting Go, Living the Dream, Sweet Pea, Sky Blue Comfrey, Red Clover, Peaceful Detachment and Speedwell.

Sweet Hunza

Prunus armeniaca (Hunza)

"Pain is resistance to feeling" Rajpur

Indications: Despair, confusion, hopelessness, feelings of failure; fighting and resisting one's experience – "Why me? Why this? Why now? When will this suffering end?"

❅

Embracing and appreciating the opportunity in the now – knowing that even in the midst of great hardship or suffering, profound healing and sweetness can be found; for finding and creating sweetness in the moment; knowing that however hard things seem to be, if we cease struggling and look for the opportunity, we will find the gift of greater understanding, greater love and healing;

Sweet Hunza teaches us that we are not victims, that at a soul level we create all our experiences, precisely for the experience and for the opportunity to grow in love and understanding. When life doesn't go according to the narrow vision of our ego/separated child self, we struggle and become agitated and fight desperately to get out of our present situation. It is this panicking, struggling and fighting that creates our suffering, not the reality of our experience, which we are trying so hard to resist. It reminds us that now is all that there is, and that out of each now moment we create our experience and beliefs – that we do have a choice – whether to run this scenario through the fight and resistance of fear, or by sitting in the embrace of peace.

Once we throw in the towel and go "Ok! I'm going to settle down and see what this really feels like, and what the opportunity is here to create healing for myself and others", then a shift occurs and things begin to make sense and suffering is transformed. Often our greatest riches, in terms of transformational understanding, arise out of what at first seemed to be the most traumatic periods in our life.

However, Sweet Hunza does not ask us to value suffering, rather it shows us that the path to peace and freedom from suffering is through the heart of our experience, by setting aside our fear and by allowing ourselves to settle down into feeling, and understanding, without judgment. It reminds us that, despite how we perceive things to be, all is well and everything is in its place, and it encourages us in the midst of challenging times, to look for opportunities to create sweet moments of healing and love, for ourselves and for others.

This essence is made from the flowers of the Hunza Apricot tree, whose native habitat is in Afghanistan and the Hunza Valley. The Hunza Apricot tree produces the smallest, most extraordinarily delicious, sweet, apricots. Hunza apricots have long been a key element in the diet of the Hunza people, who have been much studied because of their health, vitality and unusual longevity.

See also: Comfrey, Stitchwort, Cherry Plum Fruit, Red Clover, Sweet Pea, Letting Go, Crimean Snowdrop, Living the Dream.

Sweet Pea

Lathyrus odoratus

"You are loved and cherished on every dimension. Names and numbers do not matter. They do not mean anything to you. What is meaningful to you is your own heart, your own soul, your own consciousness, your own potential, your own divine beauty. But we desire you to know that you are not alone."

"Angels and guides are valid. However, know that the greater spiritual beingness of you occupies all of the dimensions simultaneously. At another level you are also angels and guides. Therefore, it is of utmost benefit if you will understand that it is, in that place of non-separation, all part of your own soul energy. Instead of calling on an outside authority, call upon the unlimited, eternal I AM. In this fashion you strengthen your own power sourceness."

P'taah The Gift – channelled by Jani King

Indications: for when we feel alone and cut off from love and spiritual support; for when we honour our angelic guides and companions, but do not recognise our own divine nature; for those who are missing the presence of loved ones who have died.

❄

Knowing that we are never alone; recognising the divine nature of all being, that we are not separate from Infinite Love, that we only separate ourselves; for connection and communion with friends in spirit, and with angels – our brothers and sisters in light; for re-uniting with our own divine essence.

As we walk through these challenging times, those in the devic and angelic realms want us to know that we do not walk alone, that they walk beside us at all times, even when we are not aware of their presence. However they do not join us in our fear or in a diminished mortal sense of ourselves, rather they encourage us to remember and to embrace our own divine stature and light – and to joyfully join them, as equal partners in the dance of the divine in all creation.

Sweet Pea essence reminds us of our true nature. In the past we have often seen our spiritual companions and guides as being greater than us in wisdom, light and love, but the time has now come for us to 'grow up' spiritually – to no longer experience ourselves as childlike 'mortals', needing to depend so much on the wisdom and loving support of seemingly greater beings. Now is the time to begin to settle deeply into the truth, wisdom and love that lies within the heart of our own being, to recognise that all that we have sought outside ourselves, lies here within us.

Over aeons of time we have separated ourselves from our own innate divine being and from the union of the divine. As we journey home, our spiritual companions rejoice with every step we take – with each affirmation of our truth, our love, our light, our true power, our divine invulnerability, our powerful creativeness and our peace.

Sweet Pea essence also reminds us that we have chosen to be here at this time in order to re-awaken divine consciousness on earth. One part of this re-awakening occurs as we begin to recognise that the earth is not separate from heaven, but is, in reality, the ever-changing creation of our combined consciousness. This creation is maintained or changed by our beliefs and perceptions, and by the response of the devas and angelic beings who over-light and integrate all life. As we change our perceptions and beliefs about ourselves, and about the nature of reality, so creation responds and this is reflected back to us by the world. Thus, in this way the very nature of the earth responds to confirm our changing consciousness.

Sweet Pea essence comforts us when loved ones have died and we miss their presence. It shows us that death is simply a movement into another dimension of being – that we can still connect with our loved ones, and feel their presence – but in a living relationship with them, as they are now, rather than as we remember them during their time here. Often we find that the bond and communion with loved ones grows stronger after they have died – and that because they are no longer limited or restricted by former emotional or physical suffering, they can now connect with us with greater love and clarity than before.

See also: One Being, Rosebay Willowherb, Divine Being, Speedwell.

The Rose

Rosa "Mme Isaac Periere"

Indications: for when we need to integrate all our many skills and qualities, in order to fulfil our life purpose at this time; for whenever we fight shy of fully expressing ourselves, for when we hold back at some level for fear of exposing ourselves; for fear of being different, unique, individual, cutting edge, or radical in what we express or in the way we express ourselves; for those whose role challenges them to openly express the light of their truth and divinity in all areas of their life.

❈

For full, true self-expression; for unfolding and integrating all the many aspects of our being, into our creativity and self-expression; for expressing our truth fully in the world; for 'Coming Out'; for the courage to be fully individual and radical in our expression and in how we create our lives; for allowing ourselves to express our true divine nature in the world and for fulfilling our incarnation role at this time; for giving our essence – our fragrance, with love, to the world.

Mme Isaac Periere is the most beautiful rose, with large fragrant blooms, made up of layers of deep rose coloured petals, each radiating like a mandala, from a golden centre. This essence was made at noon, at midsummer, and speaks to us of the zenith of our self-expression – the time when we draw on all that we are and have been so far, and give the gift of that to the world, with love, without restraint and without fear of judgement – knowing that in the resonance of that, we liberate others also to embrace and give the gift of their full expression to the world.

At this time of transition, we are moving beyond a limited sense of who we are, and of what life is, into an understanding of divine reality, divine being and divine creation. We have the opportunity to create and express our highest and widest vision. In our creative processes we can reach further than we have ever dreamed before, to draw on our finest inspiration, and integrate that within what we express and create at this time.

We can use 'The Rose' essence whenever we are reining in our self-expression out of self-consciousness or lack of confidence. It helps us to find ways to understand what it that we wish to express, how we can do so, and how we can integrate and develop all the necessary skills and resources, so that our vision can unfold. Sometimes we already have within us all that we need – and all that is required is for us to integrate these skills in order to accomplish our vision. At other times we need to develop new skills and add these to our existing palette in order to be fully equipped for what we wish to accomplish.

In common with orchid and lotus essences, rose essences often have a very wide-ranging application. It is almost as if they over-light a wide arena of our experience. They provide overarching support for the development of our understanding in this arena. 'The Rose' is no exception – it supports and nourishes the development of true and full expression, and the integration and development of all the aspects of understanding necessary for this process. As such, it is non-specific, but far-reaching. We can take it on it's own, or use it's over-lighting vision to highlight to us the more specific self-expression issues that we need to address.

See also: Honesty, Blue Delphinium, Violet, Cyclamen, At the Heart of Being, Pure Love, Living the Dream, Lilac, Speedwell, Violet, True Power, Child's Play, Reunion, Passionate Life, Celandine.

True Power

Crocus thomasinianus "Royal"

Indications: for fear of power, and fear of abuse of power; for when we avoid taking on roles of responsibility or leadership, fearing the responsibility of power; for when we attract jealousy, envy, hatred, revenge; for when we are jealous ourselves of those have power; for when we abuse or manipulate power, for power struggles and power games; for a distorted hunger for love and recognition; for feelings of powerlessness; for resolving conflict and power struggles.

❇

For realising that true power lies within us in the limitless love and truth of our being – that this is power and stature beyond measure, and can never be diminished or taken by anyone.

Over aeons of time, both here on earth, and elsewhere in the universe and multiverses, beings have struggled for external power and authority in a distorted search for that which they have separated from. Our struggles for power are none other than a desperate hunger for love and recognition, and are born out of the illusion of separation from our divine being.

True Power teaches us that there is no greater power than the power of love and truth – that true power lies within us in the infinite love and truth of our being – that this is power and stature beyond recognition – wealth and gold beyond measure. Love and truth are our birthright – they can never be diminished or taken away by another, nor can they be gained or earned outside ourselves.

True Power often arises when we feel powerless in some area of our experience. It shows us that being powerful or 'in our power' is not something that we get or acquire, rather it is being completely at peace and at one with who we are – happy to be who we are, and being congruent in our choices, so that we live who we are and what feels right for us, without being concerned about other people's opinions or judgment.

It reminds us of our essential wholeness, and the wholeness of our true and infinite self. Achievement, status, wealth, admiration, health, beauty, can all be lost in a moment. What really satisfies and gives us a sense of wholeness lies inside us, in the core of our Being. We only feel powerless when we leave this point of infinite peace and love that lies within us. We do this when we judge ourselves to be less than whole, or less than powerful in some way. True Power reminds us of who we truly are, and of the power of the love and truth of being who we are.

So long as we continue to seek for power and recognition outside ourselves we do not know the reality of true power. Power sought outside ourselves is fool's gold. In place of feeling powerful, we feel fearful, defensive, and at times aggressive, in a desperate bid to hold onto our 'power'.

These dynamics are played out on a domestic, worldwide and universal scale. The same distorted hunger for love and recognition lies behind all power struggles. The bully in the playground is acting from the insecurity of not experiencing love and true self-worth. Lust for power, money, sex, authority, recognition, food, drugs – all of these are all unrecognised attempts to fill the void in our hearts, arising from our separation from ourselves, and from the infinite love and peace of our being.

We may be called upon to take up positions of power, but may be afraid to do so, fearing the responsibility of power, and the potential for power to be abused. We may have abused power in other lifetimes, or we may have witnessed others abusing or manipulating power for their own ends. We may also be reluctant to take power, fearing that we may become the target of other people's jealousy and bad feelings.

True Power helps us to recognise when, or when not, to take on a role of responsibility and power. If we hold positions of power and responsibility, it encourages us to find ways of empowering others, by sharing power, knowledge, information and responsibility. True Power inspires us to honour our integrity, to be honest, to listen, to admit our mistakes, and to learn from them, to stand our ground when needed, and to stand aside when we have played our part.

The flowers of this crocus are a beautiful rich deep purple, with a centre of deep orange stamens. I often find that purple in flowers relates to honesty, integrity, and to healing the need for recognition and approval, and that deep orange in flowers relates to infinite love and abundance and to healing our fear of lack of love and abundance. The combination of these two colours, mirrors to me the dynamics of the healing inspiration of True Power.

See also: Blue Delphinium, Violet, Honesty, Heart Flow, Living the Dream, Loving me – Loving You, Golden Blessings, Original Innocence, Goldenrod, At the Heart of Being, Phoenix Rebirth, Yellow Hyacinth, Physostegia, Pure Love, Red Quince, Red Poppy, Blue Salvia, Inner Fire.

Violet

Viola odorata

*"...for they admonish and stir up a man to that which
is comely and honest"*
John Gerard – on the sweet violet (1597)

Indications: for those in the public eye who face the challenge of maintaining their honesty, humility, integrity and privacy; for those who avoid public exposure, fearing loss of boundaries and integrity, and fearing that their own insecure ego will be drawn into glamour; for fear of exposure.

For those in the public eye – Violet encourages them to express truth, and to maintain individual integrity, boundaries and privacy. It balances the ego, dis-empowering the glamour of 'image' creation and promoting true humility and integrity. For those who fear exposure and therefore avoid giving their gift to the world, Violet encourages them to 'come out', whilst retaining their honesty, integrity and boundaries.

Sometimes our life path takes us into the challenging world of the public arena – a world in which it becomes easy to lose our centre and integrity – increasing demands may be made on us – image and publicity agents seek to draw us into manipulating the truth – our privacy is invaded – people are attracted by our image, or jealous of our success. If we become insecure and uncentered, we may deny our integrity in order to maintain our position.

As with anything we seek outside ourselves, fame, glamour and recognition do not fill the void within. Violet essence inspires us to seek

159

only within ourselves for love and recognition. It helps us to develop true self-worth and to maintain our clarity, honesty, humility, integrity and boundaries when in the public eye.

Our soul choice may be calling us to play a public role at this time, but our limited, frightened sense of self sometimes may prefer to stay a hermit or a shrinking violet for the rest of our days, rather than take on the challenge of 'getting out there'. This may be because we are afraid that our fragile ego will be lured by the glamour. We may also fear a loss of privacy and boundaries, being devoured by the others' neediness, or our life being taken over by the fast moving demands and commercial machinations of the world. We may fear being 'seen' – and our very human-ness being exposed. We may also fear not being able to 'come up with the goods' – not having something valid to offer, or not being able to continue to offer something of value.

Violet encourages us to move beyond these fears, so that we may take our gifts out into the world, whilst staying centred in our true source of power. It inspires us to realise that it is within our very human-ness – our being real – that our true gift lies. By honouring our integrity and honesty, and by being fully conscious of our motives, we can remain responsible for what we are creating. We will also be more aware of when we need to retire from the limelight. In this way we can honour our soul's choice at this time, whilst freeing ourselves from the illusory lure and trap of glamour.

Violet flowers have a beautiful sweet perfume, which is fleeting – once smelt it is hard to detect again for a while. One element of the violet's perfume is a chemical called ionine, which temporarily deadens our smell receptors once we have smelt its fragrance. In some ways this trait is embodied in the inspiration of this essence, as well as in it's indications. If we are a 'shrinking violet' we will try to hide our fragrance from others – however, one way of surviving exposure and publicity is the ability to become invisible – to have no fixed 'identity' or 'personality' that would enable others to pin us down – to become instead, simply the movement of 'being', responding afresh moment by moment, without reference to the past or to 'who we are'.

See also: True Power, Loving Me – Loving You, Heart Flow, Physostegia, Goldenrod, Honesty, Blue Delphinium, Cyclamen, Pussy Willow, Pure Love, Yellow Hyacinth, The Rose, At the Heart of Being, Orange Wallflower, Golden Blessings, Peaceful Detachment, Inner Fire, Child's Play, Sweet Pea.

Wild Cyclamen

Cyclamen coum

Indications: for times when we don't have outside support or help from others (except from spirit); for lack of confidence in our ability to stand alone and be self-supporting and self-referring; for when we don't feel adult enough to make independent decisions, or to manage responsibility without the advice, support and approval of others; for when we don't trust our own abilities and judgement; for those who feel that they have never grown up – who have never developed adult confidence and assurance; for those who feel dis-empowered when faced with the strong opinions of others; for those who find it hard to be alone; for children who do not have sufficient support or nurture in their lives.

Wild Cyclamen relates to the un-confident child within us, who may not have had the support it needed at some point in childhood. Perhaps we had to manage alone in the world, or in threatening circumstances, without compassionate adult support and guidance. As a result, we may never have fully grown up, and may still feel somewhat powerless, naïve, and lacking in sufficient confidence to stand on our own two feet.

Perhaps we find it hard to trust our own judgment, are anxious about taking responsibility for important decisions, and frequently seek the advice or approval of others whom we perceive to be more capable than ourselves. It may be a challenge for us to stand alone in our opinions and decisions when faced with the disapproval of others, who are seemingly more confident or more experienced than ourselves.

Wild Cyclamen helps us to parent and support our inner child, so that we can grow up to become confident, self-referring, individuals, in charge of our own lives, our own affairs and our own decisions and opinions. It encourages us to quietly seek our own counsel, and to feel confident enough to trust and to follow our own judgement.

This essence inspires us to develop inner strength, solidity and knowing. These qualities are innate within us, but if we have relied too long on the opinions and support of others, we may not have developed our own abilities. It's like a muscle that hasn't been much used – the more we exercise it, the more it grows in strength and flexibility, and the more our confidence and capability grows. Wild Cyclamen connects us strongly to our intuition, our basic survival skills and our common sense. It also strengthens our awareness of our higher Self, our guides and our guardian angels.

Wild Cyclamen also relates to those children who are unsupported by the adults around them, or who face isolation from their peers. It encourages them to access their intuitive survival skills, and their innate inner parenting skills, so that they can support and care for themselves, until greater support is provided by those around them. It helps to counter the loss of confidence that might otherwise occur, and ease their sense of aloneness.

For some, (women in particular), this essence relates to the loss of a male partner, who may have provided support and counsel for many years. One may be faced with making important decisions on one's own, often with no one to ask for advice; dealing with banks, legal matters, life decisions etc. At the same time there is the experience of living alone and being on one's own for long periods, without daily companionship, perhaps for the first time in one's life.

Wild Cyclamen helps us to connect deep within ourselves to the love and the strength that lie within us. It also increases our awareness of those in spirit, who deeply love and guide us, and share with us our journey. We no longer feel so alone, but instead can begin to discover a rich, inner companionship with our friends in spirit. (See also Sweet Pea)

This essence also addresses those times when we find ourselves standing alone in relation to peers or colleagues, perhaps because we have a different way of being, different opinions, or different principles. This may attract bullying or rejection from those around us, who may feel threatened by our individuality, or by what they see as our (spoken or unspoken) judgement of them. It may re-open wounds from similar situations that we encountered in our childhood, and can leave us feeling lonely, childlike and questioning ourselves. Wild Cyclamen helps us to rebuild our confidence by inspiring us to carefully consider our own choices and opinions. It encourages us to be self-referring, self-assessing, and trusting of our own deepest judgement and instinct. (see also Goldenrod and Divine Being)

Doctrine of Signatures: Wild Cyclamen (Cyclamen coum) flowers in the coldest weather in January and February. It has deep pink flowers, tinged with magenta, which grow up through mounds of glossy dark-green, heart-shaped leaves. Cyclamen coum plants are self-supporting, and survive for many years in the harshest conditions, in shade, without watering or feeding. They do so by gradually building a reserve of food and moisture in their corm (a solid, dense, hard, heart-shaped tuber). In times of drought or low nutrition Cyclamen draws on the reserves in its corm to sustain itself.

See also: Goldenrod, Father Sun, Divine Being, True Power, At the Heart of Being, Red Poppy, Orange Wallflower, Loving Me – Loving You, Blue Delphinium, Physostegia, Honesty.

With Love

Rose "Sophie's Perpetual"

Indications: dragging ourselves through life; feeling depressed about what our life consists of; all work and no play; feeling unfulfilled, resentful and half-hearted about what we've taken on; exhaustion; feeling weighed down by trying to live and work according to social, or other, standards, structures and ideals, whether imposed on us, self-imposed or a mixture of both; for the heart chakra.

With Love is about doing what we love and loving what we do. It prompts us to look at what we choose to do with our lives – how we feel about what we have chosen to do, and if we are half-hearted about it, why, and what we can do about it. It encourages us live a life that is loving towards ourselves and others, within which we wholeheartedly love what we are doing, and do it in such a way that whatever we do is imbued with the resonance of our love.

There are many reasons why we don't always enjoy our lives and what we are doing in our days: – we may feel stressed by time-watching and dead-lines or we may feel that we are trying to keep too many plates in the air – we may be anxious about failing to meet some standard we have set ourselves or that others expect of us – we may be afraid of giving too much and having no boundaries to giving – or we may be doing things that we feel we 'ought' to do or 'have' to do, but which we hate doing or have grown away from.

With Love helps us to look at the choices we make in our lives on a daily basis, as to what we do and how we do it, and also at the bigger choices we make regarding our choice of work, relationships, whether we have children or not, where we live etc. It makes clear the reasons why we are not always wholehearted about our choices so that we become able to see what it is that we need to change in order to create a life that is, more loving, more wholehearted and more joyful for ourselves and for those around us.

Sometimes it may highlight a need for boundaries – a need to empower those around us to share the load of the daily practical things that need doing; at others, it may help us to realise our need to move on, to have more fun in our lives, to take regular time off, or to find a more comfortable, flexible and human way to do our work. Perhaps we need to reduce the amount of load we carry or we may wish to follow a long held dream, which has become an: 'if only my life were different' type of dream.

It can be helpful to combine the inspiration of With Love, with the essence Living the Dream, in order that we may have the courage and certainty to begin to live our dream for ourselves and for the world. There is a book, called "Excuse Me, Your Life is Waiting" by Lyn Grabhorn which I would recommend to anyone who finds themselves regularly saying "If only…" This book may change your view of how life works and whether it is possible to live a life that is abundant, loving, miraculous and fun.

With Love encourages us to choose to live our life in a way that is truly loving to ourselves, so that we 'have a life' and do not always carry the load for others. If we are feeling resentful of the things we do for others, or feel that we are doing more than our fair share, we can combine With Love, with Heart Mother, Inner Fire or Red Poppy, and Phoenix Rebirth, to release old anger, set boundaries, empower others and come to a point where whatever we do, we do wholeheartedly with love.

With Love encourages us to create a life that is rich and varied, relaxed and inspiring, abundant, and filled with beauty, joy and creativity. It shows us that this is our birthright – that we are not meant to create and maintain a life of suffering and drudgery for ourselves or for others. It asks us to recognise in our choices, that love works, and that if we choose to create a life that is loving towards ourselves and towards others, then the universe will support us in this. It reminds us that there is no virtue in suffering or in creating a hard life for ourselves, and that there is no healing to be found in creating an exhausting and over-demanding life.

Once we create a life that is wholehearted and loving, all that we do becomes enriched by our love. When we live With Love, the resonance of what we create, brings love, healing and inspiration to ourselves and to others. As we prepare a meal we fill it with love; when we pay our bills we do so with love and gratitude for the services and goods provided; whatever our work, no matter if it is humble or world changing, it resonates with our love and our joy – whatever we do, we do without sacrificing our health, happiness or integrity.

See also: Living the Dream, Pussy Willow, Speedwell, Disciple of the Heart, Cyclamen, Original Innocence, Inner Fire, Heart Mother, Blue Delphinium, Physostegia, Phoenix Rebirth.

Yellow Hyacinth

Hyacinth, 'City of Haarlem'

Indications: for when we have lost respect for others; despising others; for prejudice; repulsion; for when we feel superior – in defence against our own sense of inferiority and lack of self-respect; for when we close our heart to others as a result of our superior judgement; for when we are critical or judgemental of those around us; for the heart, solar plexus and brow chakras.

❉

Respect for others, knowing that we are all equal in worth, regardless of our achievements or our level of understanding or experience; allowing others room to grow and heal in our vision of them; recognising another's gifts, qualities and potential; having essential respect for others at the level of their true, divine self; 'casting out the mote in one's own eye'; treating others with impartiality.

Yellow Hyacinth addresses when we have lost respect for others and despise them because they have failed to meet some standard that we have set. Often we do this when we have put someone on a pedestal, or have held them in greater authority than ourselves, and then have sought a way to promote ourselves out of our own subsequent feelings of inferiority. This can happen when we have been needy and co-dependent in a relationship, or have denied our own worth and integrity; and subsequently, in our struggle to regain self-respect and empower ourselves, we have diminished another in our judgement (often unspoken) and closed our heart to them.

Yellow Hyacinth teaches us that we are never superior to others, that we are all equal and worthy of love and essential respect, whether we have apparently accomplished much, or seemingly very little. It shows us how to allow room in our vision of others, for growth, understanding, miracles and love – rather than measuring and fixing ourselves and others with a yardstick of small minded judgement and unrealistic expectations, which are neither loving nor true.

Often when we judge others we don't allow ourselves to recognise what their personal journey might be, or the speed or route it might need to take. We think that we know what others need to do, and how they need to do it. Impatient with others' rate of progress we do not recognise our own blind spots and 'failings', or the achievements and qualities of others. They may have faced challenges that we ourselves would find hard and they may have developed qualities that we ourselves may have neglected.

Rudolph Steiner suggests that if a teacher has a child in their class whose behaviour they find challenging; this teacher should work silently on a similar dynamic within his or her own personality, and through this, energetically prompt a shift in the consciousness of the child. Often the traits which disturb us most in others are those traits which we have not yet fully dealt with in ourselves. Yellow Hyacinth demonstrates how those around us, often mirror back to us the very issues and patterns that we have not yet fully resolved in ourselves.

We know that when others treat us with respect for our equal self-worth, and potential, it allows us to express and to develop the best in ourselves, free from the limitations of judgement. When we let go of our negative perceptions of another person, this creates a positive expansion of vision, which is sensed energetically by that one, and offers them the space to expand into more of their potential and healing. This can be seen in the miracles that often occur, following powerful, positive absent healing or prayer. (Yellow Hyacinth can be taken in conjunction with Child's Play and Peaceful Detachment, as a preparation for sending absent healing.)

See also: Beauty in the Eye, Phoenix Rebirth, Red Poppy, Original Innocence, Pink Cherry, Heart Flow, Pure Love, True Power, Celandine, Red Quince.

Light Heart

Flower Essence Combinations

❄

These essence combinations have been put together to address the dynamics of particular issues in our lives. These combinations are deliberately detailed in their make-up, in order to take into account the various strands of our lives and our beliefs, that influence how we respond to different situations and to different experiences.

Peace in a Storm

❊

For staying centred and peaceful in a crisis: for peaceful, appropriate response, unaffected by the drama and trauma of events around us; for stillness and connection to the moment; for understanding and embracing strong emotions (one's own or others), without feeling overwhelmed or afraid; for gentle release of tension, fear, shock, anger or grief.

Indications: for panic, shock or extreme emotion; for tension and worry; for whenever we become un-centred – reacting blindly, or frozen in our response; for fear of breakdown or collapse; for support in stressful situations – travelling, dental or hospital visits, accidents, operations etc.

Peace in a Storm contains:
Crimean Snowdrop: for healing the memory of shock and trauma

Speedwell: for alert, centred focus; for being fully present and connected in the moment

Stitchwort: for staying in our peace and not 'jumping out' in shock or fear

Peaceful Detachment: for peaceful detachment from the emotional drama and trauma of events around us and in the world – seeing things from a divine perspective.

Red Clover: for panic – for settling into our heart of peace.

Sweet Hunza: for when we despair; for finding purpose and teaching in the midst of difficult experiences.

Cherry Plum Fruit: for peacefully embracing strong emotions, without judgement or fear.

Physostegia: for not being swayed by other people's emotional or ego dynamics; for centering, and checking in with oneself to know how to respond to a situation.

Red Poppy: for taking positive action, not being a victim.

Divine Being: for when we feel vulnerable or dis-empowered by a situation, for remembering our divine invulnerability.

At the Heart of Being: for connecting to our timeless infinite Being.

Sweet Pea: for knowing we are never alone and are always supported by those in spirit who love and care for us.

Take Time

❄

Take time to be, take time to connect, take time to play, take time to really look and see, take time to listen, take time to enjoy, take time to eat well, take time to rest and relax, take time to do the things you've always wanted to do, take time to look after yourself, take time to think, take time to do something well, take time to love, take time to live!

Situation: for when we go too fast, rushing ahead without connecting to now; feeling like we've never enough time; too much doing and never being; feeling crowded out of the picture – no longer in charge of one's own time – no time to rest or to care for oneself, no time to play or to follow one's interests.

Take Time contains:
Speedwell: for stepping into timelessness – making the most of each moment – taking the time to connect, to really look, see, listen and feel – for taking the time of one's life and really enjoying it.

Cyclamen: self-nurture – for making the time and space to care for oneself; for nurturing one's body, mind and soul – one's core energy and dreams.

Bluebell Grove: for taking time to deeply relax and rest in order to restore one's energy and spirit.

Cherry Plum Fruit: for taking time to connect with how one is feeling.

Grandmothers Arms: for living at a comfortable, sustainable pace; for understanding what heals.

Child's Play: for taking time to play and have fun, and to laugh and be joyful.

The Rose: for integrating all our skills, experience and capabilities.

Pink Cherry: for loving and cherishing ourselves and others, for allowing softness and beauty into our life.

Passionate Life: for courage, motivation; zest for life, adventurousness – overcoming obstacles and setbacks.

Living the Dream: for positively living our dream for ourselves and for the world.

Heart Mother: for when we spend too much time picking up the pieces for others and not enough time looking after our own needs.

Self Worth

❄

For loving and understanding ourselves; for having the courage to speak out, and to stand our ground; for valuing our own and understanding and instincts, and for taking steps to bring about positive change in our life.

Indications: loss of confidence and integrity; feeling crushed by another's judgement; feeling a victim; for when we give way to outside influences, authority figures or peer group pressure;

Self Worth contains:
Red Poppy: for a fiery sense of self-worth; for constructive use of anger to bring about positive change; for setting boundaries without guilt.

Goldenrod: for peaceful assertion, inner authority, self-respect; for following one's own instincts and understanding.

At the Heart of Being: for connecting to the deep peace and wisdom of one's core self.

Blue Salvia: for seeing clearly the truth of a situation, behind the mask or the smokescreen.

Physostegia: for not being swayed by other people's emotional or ego dynamics; for centering, and checking in with oneself to know how to respond to a situation.

At the Heart of Being: for connection to our timeless divine self.

Blue Delphinium: for speaking out with honesty and integrity, listening for the words to say and for when to speak.

Red Quince: being 'big enough' to hear the truth in what others say; for when we react painfully and defensively to what others say.

Original Innocence: for holding ourselves in the light of innocence: for guilt and feelings of imperfection;

Loving Me, Loving You: for feeling relaxed and happy with who we are, enjoying our uniqueness; being warm and loving towards ourselves and others.

Passionate Life: for courage, motivation; zest for life, adventurousness – overcoming obstacles and setbacks.

Lighter Space

Space Clearing essence

✳

Lighter Space can be used daily to lighten and revitalise the atmosphere of the home or the workplace, bringing a breath of fresh air and uplifting 'chi' energy. Where there has been upset or trauma, prolonged computer use, or a build up of negative depressed energy, this light, powerful blend of essences will renew the positive energy of a place, clearing and transforming negative resonance and accumulated electromagnetic energy.

Lighter Space clears and lightens the energy of buildings, accident or conflict spots, jewellery, furniture, fabrics, and crystals. Use to clear the energy of a new home or workspace, or to create a light, peaceful atmosphere in hotel rooms.

Lighter Space contains:
Original Innocence: for a return to innocence and purity, a release of judgement and guilt.

Crimean Snowdrop: for healing the memory of trauma and suffering, wherever it is held, in our being, in an environment or in material objects.

Peaceful Detachment: for peaceful detachment from other people's negative emotional energy and drama; for holding others in the light of their highest potential and healing.

Celandine: for joy and light, celebrating the joy and light of the divine in all.

178

Child's Play: for lightening up our life with joy, laughter, and innocent fun and play.

Divine Being: for when we feel vulnerable to outside influences – viruses, radiation, other people's emotional and psychic energy etc. – reminds us that we are powerful divine energy beings creating our reality through what we think and believe.

Living the Dream: for moving beyond trust and hope into empowerment and positive action that affirms our choice to create heaven on earth, now, at this time.

One Being: for being deeply centred and at one with oneself and the infinite peace of the one 'Being' – the divine in all.

Green Alexanders: for connection to the freshness and uplifting vitality of natural 'chi' energy.

Sweet Pea: for experiencing the loving and supportive presence of our brothers and sisters in light – angels, guides and friends in spirit.

Make Love

Sensual Loving essence

For passionate, open-hearted, tender, playful loving. Brings a deep enjoyment of male and female sexuality and our individual physiques, encouraging us to love and appreciate ourselves just as we are, and to share the gift of our loving, tenderly and playfully with our partner, savouring each moment and each touch as we create a deep and loving connection.

Make Love contains:
Red Gladiolus: for celebration and appreciation of women's sexuality; for honouring our integrity in relation a to the choices we make around how we use our sexuality.

Horse Chestnut Leaf Bud: for celebration and appreciation of men's physicality and sexuality.

Pink Cherry: for unconditional tender love: for gentle sensitive touch.

Loving Me, Loving You: for relaxed enjoyment of our individual and unique beauty.

Speedwell: for taking time to really savour and enjoy each moment and each touch.

Heart Flow: for opening our hearts – letting go of defence.

Pure Love: for shifting from wanting to be loved – to being the lover – loving oneself and others.

Beauty in the Eye: for seeing the true beauty of our partner.

Child's Play: for playful, light-hearted loving.

Sleep Well

❄

For deep, peaceful rest and relaxation – reassures and settles a busy, fearful, or worried mind, encouraging us to let go of emotional tension and restlessness, so that we feel relaxed and secure enough to sleep. Can also be used to centre and ground us whenever we are in an over-active or over-excited state of mind.

Sleep Well contains:
Bluebell Grove: for making the time and space for deep rest and relaxation.

Speedwell: for settling deeply and peacefully into the moment, not pulled forward by concerns about the future and not drawn back by past events.

Cyclamen: for taking care of one's energy and wellbeing; building a core of energy and vitality through rest and care of one's physical and emotional needs.

Pussy Willow: for going with the flow of life – with what is truly comfortable and appropriate, with our inner rhythms and real sense of timing.

Sky Blue Comfrey: for connection to the infinite, deep peace of our being.

Grandmothers Arms: for living life at a sustainable and healing pace.

Crimean Snowdrop: for healing the memory of trauma and suffering.

Letting Go: for letting go, and gentle transformation of deep fears in the human psyche.

Red Clover: deeply settles and reassures us that all is well – for whenever we are panicky, anxious or worried.

Peaceful Detachment: for peaceful detachment from other people's emotional drama; holding others in the light of their highest potential and healing.

Sweet Pea: for experiencing the loving and supportive presence of angels, guides and friends in spirit.

Working Harmony

Office and Study essence

❈

For offices, workplaces, classrooms, group work, as well as for study and exam preparation.

In the workplace or study environment, *Working Harmony* encourages centred focus and attention to detail, as well as awareness of the bigger picture. It helps us develop intuitive, creative ways to manage complex situations and multi-level information, without feeling overwhelmed, and it inspires us to find flexible, sustainable ways of working that respond to our creativity and to the real timing of life and events. In this way our work becomes play and our play inspires our work.

Working Harmony creates greater harmony and co-operation amongst members of a group, encouraging us to stay centred in our interactions with others, so that we can respond peacefully and appropriately without being affected by other people's emotional or ego dynamics. It encourages us to honour our own integrity and understanding, whilst remaining open and willing to listen to other people's points of view.

Working Harmony contains:
Physostegia: for not being swayed by other people's emotional or ego dynamics; for centering, and checking in with oneself to know how to respond to a situation.

Goldenrod: for peaceful assertion, inner authority, self-respect; for following one's own instincts and understanding.

Red Quince: for being 'big enough' to hear the truth in what others say; for when we react painfully and defensively to another's comments and suggestions.

Speedwell: for deep, peaceful, centred focus in the moment; for attention to detail and enjoyment of doing things carefully; for taking time and not rushing.

Pussy Willow: for going with the flow and developing flexible ways of working that respond to the true timing of life and events.

Lilac: for managing complex tasks and multi-level information without overwhelm.

Child's Play: for imagination, playful creativity and fun – finding ways to turn work into play.

Disciple of the Heart: for finding heart-impelled ways of creating structure, discipline, self-discipline and standards.

Yellow Hyacinth: for self-respect and respect for others – allowing room in our perception for others to grow and change.

Reunion: for integrating linear and lateral perspectives in one's work and understanding.

Blue Delphinium: for the courage to speak out, for speaking, writing and singing; for developing the ability to listen to others, as well as for the words to say or to write; for knowing when to speak.

Red Poppy: for self-esteem; for using anger constructively to bring about positive change.

Wild Cyclamen: for developing the skills and resourcefulness to stand on one's own two feet in the world; for dealing with, and understanding, money, the law, business and structure.

At One

Meditation Essence

❋

For deep stillness – being deeply *At One* with ourselves and with life; for a timeless sense of 'being', and 'being with' the world. *At One* can be used to deepen our meditation, and to heighten our awareness and connection to the moment, and to understanding. It is grounding and centering, and can be used whenever we wish to become more mindful or aware. Used regularly it can help us to become more meditative and aware at all times.

At One contains:
At the Heart of Being: for connection to the deep stillness and wisdom of one's essential being.

One Being: for being at one with the spirit and energy of all things and all beings; for grounded expansion of awareness and the development of clairvoyant, clairaudient and clairsentient awareness.

Reunion: for integration of multi-dimensional awareness; for letting go our fear of expanded awareness.

Speedwell: for timeless awareness; for expanding fully into each timeless moment, for deep, still, peaceful attention.

Self Healing

❄

For inspiring confidence in our ability to heal; for letting go our fear of illness; for letting go our feelings of guilt or imperfection in relation to health; for taking good care of ourselves; for awareness of what heals our body, mind and soul.

Indications: for lack of confidence in our ability to heal, feelings of powerlessness, guilt or failure in relation to illness or injury.

Self Healing contains:
Divine Being: for when we feel vulnerable to outside influences – viruses, illness, radiation, other people's emotional and psychic energy etc. – reminds us that we are powerful divine energy beings creating our reality through what we think and believe.

Crab Apple Fruit: for letting go of any feelings of imperfection or guilt in relation to our health.

Stitchwort: for shock; feelings of acute vulnerability and sensitivity; fear of living; for not 'jumping out' in shock or fear – helps us to ground the light of who we are fully into our body; brings joy in living in a 'physical world'.

Crimean Snowdrop: for healing the memory of shock and trauma.

Cyclamen: for taking good care of one's health and wellbeing.

Pink Cherry: soothes and comforts when we need gentleness and TLC.

Letting Go: for gentle letting go of deep fear.

Pussy Willow: for flexibility and connection to the real flow and timing of life.

Comfrey: for dynamic patience; recognising and embracing the gift within our present experience; for when we fight and resist our present situation or feel limited or restricted by it.

Sky Blue Comfrey: for infinite, dynamic peace; coming into the timelessness of each moment of our infinite being.

Green Alexanders: for connecting to the revitalising and uplifting 'chi' energy of the natural world and the elements; for enjoyment of movement and physical exercise.

Red Clover: for not panicking and not worrying; for settling down into our peace.

Passionate Life: for courage, motivation; zest for life, adventurousness – overcoming obstacles and setbacks.

Red Poppy: for not being a victim; taking positive action to improve our situation.

Speedwell: for taking the time that we need to heal and to care for ourselves properly.

Grandmothers Arms: for living life at a sustainable pace; for connection to the healing spirit in nature and the elements.

Living the Dream: for moving beyond trust and hope into empowerment and positive action that affirms our choice to create heaven on earth, now, at this time.

True Beauty

❄

To remind us that true beauty shines from within, from the love that we are, and from the love that we give to ourselves and to others.

The essences in *True Beauty* remind us to be happy to be who we are, and inspire us to let go our judgement about how we look, or about how 'nice' a person we might be. In loving and understanding ourselves, and being happy to be real, we allow our true light and beauty to shine to the world.

True Beauty contains:
Loving Me – Loving You: for feeling relaxed and happy with who we are, enjoying our uniqueness; being warm and loving towards ourselves and others.

Crab Apple Fruit: for letting go of any feelings of imperfection or guilt in relation to our body or our looks.

Pink Cherry: soothing; for being gentle and loving towards ourselves and towards others.

Original Innocence: for holding ourselves in the light of innocence.

Honesty: for being happy to be real, and to show our true face and our humanness.

Divine Being: for when we feel vulnerable to outside influences – viruses, illness, radiation, other people's emotional and psychic energy etc.

Sky Blue Comfrey: for fear of aging – for coming into the timelessness of each moment of our infinite being.

Heart of Peace

For peaceful detachment from the drama and trauma of world events or of events around us; for restoring a sense of proportion, peace, happiness and safety; for realising that by choosing peace in place of fear, we create an environment for peace and safety, and appropriate response – in our own lives and also in the world.

Indications: panic, anxiety and worry; for whenever we are affected by mass fear of attack, fear of disease, or fear of environmental or financial disaster; for when we feel anxious, as though something bad might happen to us, or to our loved ones, but we don't know what; for when we worry about the health, finances or personal security of loved ones, or of ourselves.

Heart of Peace contains:
Red Clover: deeply settles and reassures us that all is well – for whenever we are panicky, anxious or worried.

Peaceful Detachment: for peaceful detachment from the emotional drama and trauma of events around us, or in the world.

Crimean Snowdrop: for healing the memory of shock and trauma.

Living the Dream: for peacefully and positively living our dream for ourselves and for the world.

Divine Being: for when we feel vulnerable to attack, or to outside influences or disease – reminds us that we are powerful divine energy beings creating our reality through what we think and believe.

Sweet Pea: for experiencing the loving support of angels, guides and friends in spirit.

Sky Blue Comfrey: for connection to the infinite, deep peace of our being.

Sweet Hunza: for when we despair; for finding purpose and teaching in the midst of difficult experiences.

Passionate Life

❄

For energy, enthusiasm, courage, joy, adventurousness, assertiveness, motivation, zest for life and new experiences; being passionately alive; overcoming obstacles and setbacks; rebuilding confidence and resilience after illness and setbacks.

Indications: for whenever we need a boost to our courage and confidence; for fear of risks and challenges; for lack of motivation, discouragement, disheartenment, hopelessness; feeling a victim of circumstance; fear of living, timidity, being over-protective of oneself; living a narrow existence out of fear.

Passionate Life *contains:*
Passionate Life: for courage, motivation; zest for life, adventurousness – overcoming obstacles and setbacks.

Letting Go: for letting go, and gentle transformation of deep fears in the human psyche.

Child's Play: for light-heartedness, imaginative creativity, playing and having fun.

The Rose: for drawing together and using all our skills, experience and capabilities.

Wild Cyclamen: for developing the skills and resourcefulness to stand on one's own two feet in the world; for dealing with, and understanding, money, the law, business and structure.

Living the Dream: for moving beyond trust and hope, into empowerment and positive action to realise our dream at this time.

Green Alexanders: for connecting to the revitalising and uplifting 'chi' energy of the natural world and the elements; for enjoyment of movement and physical exercise.

Heart Mother: for when we spend too much time picking up the pieces for others and not enough time looking after our own needs.

With Love: for wholeheartedness; for understanding why we are not always wholehearted about our life or work; for listening to our heart, and choosing from the heart.

Forgiveness

❄

For forgiveness and self-forgiveness: for letting go old anger, judgement, self-judgement and guilt; for compassion and deep understanding of ourselves and of others; for moving out of patterns of powerlessness and being a victim.

Indications: for healing relationships where there is much anger, old hurt, judgement and grievances, which it seems impossible to clear and forgive; for guilt and self-judgement; for when we see ourselves as the victim in situations and in relationships.

Forgiveness *contains:*
Phoenix Rebirth: for letting go the judgment we hold against ourselves and others; for moving out of patterns of powerlessness and being a victim.

Original Innocence: for letting go of deep guilt and self-judgement.

Blue Delphinium: for speaking out with honesty and integrity, for listening for the words to say and for when to speak.

Red Poppy: for a fiery sense of self-worth; for constructive use of anger to bring about positive change; for setting boundaries without guilt.

Pink Cherry: for softening and opening our heart, to ourselves and to others.

Yellow Hyacinth: for respect for ourselves and for others – for allowing ourselves and others the room in our perception to grow and change.

Red Deadnettle: for the pain, anger and bitterness of rejection; for re-opening our hearts to loving ourselves and others; for seeing our part in the story.

Red Quince: being 'big enough' to hear the truth in what others say; for when we react painfully and defensively to what others say.

Healing Grief

❄

For embracing the full range of our grief, peacefully, without judgement; for uncovering the healing that lies at the heart of grief; for making the time and space to grieve, and for caring for oneself in the process; for healing the memory of trauma and suffering; for forgiveness, connection to spirit and new beginnings.

Indications: for the grief and broken-heartedness of bereavment or relationship break-up; for the shock and trauma of loss; for unresolved anger, bitterness and guilt; for unfinished grieving; for loss of confidence after loss or rejection.

Healing Grief *contains:*
Cherry Plum Fruit: for peacefully embracing strong emotions, without judgement or fear.

Sweet Hunza: for despair and hopelessness, knowing that fruit will be borne out of our experience however hard it may seem at the time; creating sweetness in the moment.

Cyclamen: for taking care of ourselves in the midst of grief – caring for our body, mind and soul.

Wild Cyclamen: learning how to cope on our own and support ourselves, and manage our own affairs.

Original Innocence: for letting go of feelings of regret, guilt and self-judgement.

Heart Flow: for keeping our heart open, allowing our feelings to flow.

Crimean Snowdrop: for healing the memory of shock and trauma.

Red Deadnettle: for the pain, anger and bitterness of rejection; for re-opening our hearts to loving ourselves and others; for seeing our part in the story.

Sweet Pea: for knowing we are never alone and are always supported by those in spirit who love and care for us.

Phoenix Rebirth: for letting go the judgment we hold against ourselves and others; for moving through anger and tears to new beginnings.

Passionate Life: for new beginnings; refinding one's zest and enthusiasm for life.

Self Expression

❄

For releasing inhibition about expressing oneself fully whether physically, vocally, creatively, or through how one lives one's life; for letting go the fear of being judged; encourages expressiveness in art, dance, singing, acting, writing etc.

Indications: for whenever we feel inhibited about expressing ourselves at any level; for stage fright and pre-speech nerves; for fear of speaking out and expressing one's true feelings.

Self Expression *contains:*

Blue Delphinium: for speaking out with honesty and integrity, for listening for the words to say and for when to speak; for letting go of inhibitions around singing and speaking.

Honesty: for being happy to show our true face and our true feelings and human-ness.

Heart Flow: for keeping our heart open, and allowing our feelings and expression to flow.

Cyclamen: for making the time and space to nurture one's talents, creativity and dreams.

The Rose: for drawing together and using all our skills, experience and capabilities in what we're trying to create.

Passionate Life: for courage, motivation; zest for life, adventurousness – overcoming obstacles and setbacks.

Celandine: for joyful self-expression, for expression of joy in words, and through singing.

Loving Me, Loving You: for feeling relaxed and happy with who we are, enjoying our uniqueness; being warm and loving towards ourselves and others.

Living the Dream: for moving beyond trust and hope, into empowerment and positive action to realise our dream at this time.

Sexual Healing

❅

For healing both men's and women's experience of sexuality; for expressing unconditional love, integrity and embodiment of spirit through sexuality; for celebration and love of both male and female sexuality.

Indications: for men and women, of whatever sexual orientation, who have experienced a split between the spiritual expression of love and sexuality and their actual physical and emotional experience – this split may have arisen from experiences of sexual trauma and abuse, sexual acts devoid of love and sensitivity, or as a response to images of male and female sexuality; for those who lack confidence in their sexuality.

Sexual Healing *contains:*
Red Gladiolus: for clarity about our original motivation and choice to enter into a sexual relationship; for celebration and appreciation of women's physicality and sexuality.

Horse Chestnut Leaf Bud: for celebration and appreciation of male physicality and sexuality.

Honesty: for honesty and willingness to show one's true face, true feelings and human-ness.

Loving Me, Loving You: for feeling relaxed and happy with who we are, enjoying our uniqueness; being warm and loving towards ourselves and others.

Crab Apple Fruit: for letting go of deep feelings of guilt, imperfection and impurity in relation to one's body and one's sexuality.

Beauty in the Eye: for seeing the true beauty of our partner.

Blue Delphinium: for losing our inhibitions around discussing our sexual relationship with our partner – helps one to listen for the words to say and for when to speak.

Pure Love: for shifting from wanting to be loved – to being the lover – loving oneself and others.

Pink Cherry: for tenderness, sensitivity and gentle, unconditional love.

Phoenix Rebirth: for letting go the judgment we hold against ourselves and others; for moving out of patterns of powerlessness and being a victim.

Women's Balance

❄

Encourages women to be kind to themselves, and to take care of their own emotional well-being and balance; inspires women to live life from the heart, and to honour their own integrity, and their need for nurture, creativity, peace, relaxation, rest, fulfilment, and fun.

Indications: for women who neglect their own needs, who need to find a balance between meeting outside demands, and caring for themselves; for resentment, tiredness and mood swings; for women who have lost their individual sense of self, and self-worth.

Womankind *contains:*
Cyclamen: for self-nurture; for making the time and space to care for oneself, and to nurture one's talents, creativity and dreams.

Heart Mother: for maintaining a balance between giving to others and giving to ourselves; for not always 'picking up the pieces' for others.

Pussy Willow: for flexibility born out of responding to the flow in life, to what is truly comfortable and appropriate; for knowing that life supports us if we support and honour ourselves.

Grandmothers Arms: for living life at a sustainable pace; for understanding what heals.

Red Quince: for emotional reactivity and sensitivity to judgement and criticism.

Red Poppy: for constructive use of anger to bring about positive change;

for setting boundaries without guilt.

Red Gladiolus: for celebration and appreciation of women's physicality and sexuality.

Sky Blue Comfrey: for fear of aging; for coming into timeless in each moment.

Bluebell Grove: for taking time out for deep rest and relaxation, to restore one's energy and spirit.

Living the Dream: for moving beyond trust and hope, into empowerment and positive action to create a life that is loving towards ourselves.

Light Heart Space

Personal Space Clearing essence

For clearing and infusing our personal energy field with light; for peaceful detachment from the emotional drama and trauma of others; for maintaining appropriate boundaries, for knowing when to give, and when to empower others to 'pick up their pieces'; for making the time and space to restore our energy and spirit; for greater clarity and understanding of what's going on in a situation or with others.

Indications: for over-sensitivity to other people's emotional drama and energy; for when are too empathic, and give too much, neglecting our own needs and energy; for when we feel drained by others; for when we become confused by mixed messages from others; for healers and therapists who need to maintain healthy boundaries.

Light Heart Space *contains:*
Peaceful Detachment: for staying peacefully detached from the emotional drama and trauma of others; for connecting to others at the level of their highest potential.

Physostegia: for staying centred, and unswayed by other people's emotional or ego dynamics; for taking time to check in to see how best to respond to a situation.

Red Poppy: for setting boundaries; for peaceful assertion; for the ability to say no.

Heart Mother: for knowing when to give, and when to empower others to 'pick up their own pieces'.

Cyclamen: for self-nurture; for making the time and space to care for oneself, and to restore one's core energy and well-being.

Divine Being: for when we feel vulnerable to outside influences – viruses, radiation, other people's emotional and psychic energy etc. – reminds us that we are powerful divine energy beings creating our reality through what we think and what we believe.

One Being: for greater clarity of understanding about what's going on in a situation or with others.

Blue Salvia: for seeing the truth behind the mask or smokescreen, seeing through confusion or mixed messages.

Sweet Pea: for awareness of support and guidance from spiritual companions and guides.

Infinite Abundance

❄

For feeling blessed; for deep appreciation of the abundance and gifts in our lives; for knowing that life supports us when we support and honour ourselves; for making the most of our resources, gifts, and skills in order to realise our dream for ourselves and for the world; for recognising that we have all that we need, exactly when we need it.

Indications: for whenever we do not recognise how blessed we are; for fear of lack; for whenever we doubt whether we can live our dream for ourselves and for the world; for when we doubt whether life will support us if we do what feels right and comfortable for us; for whenever we block the flow of giving and receiving in our lives.

Infinite Abundance contains:
Golden Blessings: for feeling blessed; for recognising the rich abundance of our life and experience.

Celandine: for joyful appreciation, and celebration of the wonders of life.

Cyclamen: for making the time and space to nurture one's creativity, talents and dreams.

Heart Mother: for managing our resources; for creating a balance between giving and receiving.

Pussy Willow: for knowing that life supports us, if we support and honour ourselves.

Wild Cyclamen: for developing the skills and resourcefulness to stand on our own two feet in the world; for dealing with, and understanding, money, the law, business and structure.

Red Poppy: for taking steps to bring about positive change in our life.

Living the Dream: for moving beyond trust and hope, into empowerment and positive action to realise our dream for ourselves and for the world; for knowing that love does prevail.

What are Flower Essences?

❄

Flower essences are like bottled spiritual healing. They inspire us to love and understand ourselves and others, to value what is real, and to develop our full potential. Through the action of light and the intention and care of the essence maker, the energetic resonances of flowers, plants, trees, crystals and light, are instilled in spring water and then preserved with brandy or vodka. Only plants and trees growing in unpolluted habitats or organic gardens are used in this process. These original tinctures (mother tinctures) are then greatly diluted before use, to ensure absolute purity and safety.

Containing only vibrational resonances, flower essences are completely safe for people of all ages and conditions, as well as for animals. Flower essences have no known side effects and can be used safely alongside both conventional and complementary treatment.

Dr Edward Bach, a medical doctor, homoeopath and immunologist, developed the first modern flower essences in Britain in the 1920s. Today, flower essences are used widely throughout the world – to inspire and empower both adults and children to cope with the emotional, mental and spiritual challenges of their lives. They are also widely used with animals.

Flower essences are energy medicine. They are not homoeopathic remedies, nor are they herbal or aromatherapy preparations, since they contain no physical component of the plants or elements involved in their making (only their energetic resonances). On a physical level they contain simply spring water, plus alcohol, or vegetable glycerine, (to act as a preservative).

On an energetic level, flower essences contain the vibrational resonances of plants or elements, together with the intentional resonances of the essence maker, and the inspirational resonances of those in spirit (devas, angels, guides) who join in the creation of each essence.

In action, they are fluid, living, messages of love and truth, which interact with each person and with their individual perceptions and awareness. They speak to us of the many aspects of love and truth, and they address those areas of our life and experience in which we do not recognise love and truth. In all of these areas they show us our one fundamental choice – the choice between love and fear – whether we buy into the illusion of fear – the 'What if?' – or the truth of Love – the 'What is'.

Flower essences help us to know and understand ourselves better. They both inspire our understanding, as well as highlight to us the dynamics of issues we are addressing. In this way we become more understanding and compassionate towards ourselves and others, as well as more aware of our negative patterns and beliefs, and how these affect our experience of life, ourselves and our relationships.

As we draw on the inspiration of flower essences, we become able to recognise and embrace all the twists and turns of our feelings, and why we react to certain situations in certain ways. As we become more self-knowing and aware, we begin to experience ourselves as the authors and creators of our lives and experiences. We no longer see ourselves as victims of circumstance, tossed about by the waves of life, or by the waves of our own or other people's emotional reactions, but learn instead, to find within ourselves all that we previously sought outside ourselves. As we begin to fill the void within – like the prodigal son, we return home – to ourselves and to our innate love, innocence, wisdom and wholeness, and to the true power of the love and truth of our being.

Flower essences are a gift at this time, offering us profound understanding and insight. How much, or in what way, we choose to draw on their inspiration, is up to each of us as individuals. We can use them occasionally, when in crisis, or we can work with them on a daily basis, over long periods of time in order to shift deep-rooted patterns, or to bring us to a powerful awareness of our true nature. Their greater purpose, if we choose to embrace it, is the recognition of the divine in all things and all beings – an end to suffering – and the remembrance and re-creation of heaven on earth – enlightenment is just a by-product of this awakening process!

How these Essences were made

❋

There are many different ways in which essence makers create flower essences. Most essence makers take as their starting point, the Sun Method that Dr Edward Bach devised, when he made his original Bach Flower Remedies in Britain, in the 1920s. This method (on a purely physical level), involves taking a clear, glass bowl, filled with pure spring water, and completely covering the surface of the water with perfect flowers, carefully picked from the plant/s for that particular essence.

This bowl of flowers is then left in full, unclouded, sunlight for about 3 hours, or until the flowers begin to wilt. The resulting 'mother' tincture is filtered, bottled with an equal proportion of 40% brandy, and then stored in a cool, dark cupboard until use. This method is still used today by essence makers who are re-creating the Bach Flower Remedies. (They also use a second method – the Boiling Method, which is particular to the making of certain of the Bach Flower Remedies).

Most essence makers today, have adapted the original Sun Method to suit their own intuitive way of working, and the individual requirements of each essence and the conditions in which that essence is made. Some essence makers no longer pick the flowers or plant parts used in the creation of an essence. Many essence makers work not only with plants, but also with crystals, elements, animal spirits, environments, and sometimes solely with light and prayer and intention.

In some way, most essence makers recognise the role of 'spirit', in the creation of an essence. Some talk in terms of God and the Divine, others in terms of angels, the devas of different plants or environments, the spirits of animals, the essence maker's guides and companions in spirit, and the spirit and intention of the maker. Almost all would agree that the pure intention and care of the essence maker, and their individual responsibility towards their work and their own emotional and spiritual wellbeing and clarity, are fundamental to the creation of essences that hold a high and pure vibrational, healing resonance.

The Creation of the Light Heart Essences:

I first began working with flower essences thirty-three years ago, and they have been an integral part of my life and journey ever since. Alongside my journey with flower essences has run my involvement with spiritual healing over the last twenty-two years. I became involved with spiritual healing primarily for my own healing and understanding, and later as an integral part of my work with clients.

I first began making these essences 11 years ago, and since then they have taken me on a profound journey in my own life, understanding and awareness. Much of this journey has been fuelled by a search for answers to all my questions of 'why?', 'what is this?', 'what will heal?', 'how do we embrace all of who we are?', 'who or what are we?', 'what is real?', etc. Some of the journey has been extremely challenging – always it has inspired me and stretched my perception of myself, of others, of the world, and of the nature of reality.

Each essence is a surprise and a revelation. I never know when I am going to make an essence. It is not something that I can command or plan in advance. It is a process that I am obedient to, and that I have learnt to trust, and to not attempt to engineer with my 'little' mind, or my limited perception of when and how and what. Whenever I make an essence it is always as a response to a kick in the pants, and a sense of 'Oh right! – Yes OK!' When I get the kick it's always obvious and the timing is always far better than I could have engineered.

Often, for several weeks before making an essence, I become intensely aware of a particular emotional and/or mental pattern or dynamic. This can be in my own experience, as well as reflected back to me by the experience of clients, members of my family, colleagues and friends. My way of dealing with this is to try to come to some kind of understanding of this dynamic by asking questions: 'What is really going on?' – 'Why do we react like this?' – 'What's the teaching in this?' – 'How can we heal this suffering?'- 'What do we need to understand in order to move out of this pattern?' I won't even be thinking about making an essence, or about what it might say if I did.

A plant may be drawing my attention, but for some reason I don't often make the connection between the plant and this search for answers, – then, one day, out of the blue, I will suddenly understand the connection between this plant, and my questions, and I will realise just what it's teaching is – what it's telling us. This often happens just after I wake in the morning, and it comes as a stream of consciousness – a flow of words and images, pouring through my mind, and suddenly I understand, and I realise that I am going to make an essence from this plant, and why, and what it's going to show us. Sometimes I make the essence that day, sometimes I have to wait a few days.

I am aware that I am certainly not capable of making a flower essence, just by using my everyday 'little' mind, or by simply carrying out the physical act of floating some flowers on the surface of a glass bowl, full of spring water, and then leaving it in the sun. Every essence maker is different in the way they work. For me, I feel as though I am one part of a team, only with the rest of the team in spirit, and not in an actual physical form here on earth at this time. Therefore, my job, (as agent Earth!) is to respond to my higher self, and to the intentions of the rest of the team and to actually carry out the physical act of making an essence, and next to understand and interpret it's inspiration and teaching (as best I can). In the process of making and working with these essences, my own understanding and perceptions are always challenged and stretched beyond their former limitations. I am deeply grateful for this process, and for the revelations and new awareness it brings.

I have never tried to identify the others members of the team, since it feels far more important to me, to listen, and to respond to their inspiration and understanding, and to focus on that in the creation of an essence, rather than to go down the distracting route of identities. What matters to me is the message, and not the messenger. However, I am increasingly aware of their presence, and their teaching and inspiration, and feel continually blessed by their unconditional love and support.

The actual methods I use vary according to the requirements of each essence. Like most essence makers, I use a clear glass bowl and pure spring water (although the Inner Fire essence was made using a bowl full of pure brandy). Mostly I am working with flowers, plants or trees, and sometimes with crystals or environmental influences (the sun, moon, stars, weather, place etc.). Three of the Light Heart Essences: Child's Play. Original Innocence and Living the Dream, were made solely with light and intention.

Sometimes with the flower essences I float the flowers on the surface of the bowl (see the Red Poppy card), and follow the Sun Method. Other times, I place the bowl within the energy field of the plant or the tree. Some essences I leave overnight, so that they are made over a 24-hour period. However I make an essence, I never plan the method, or the timing beforehand, but always wait until the actual event, and then follow what feels appropriate and right for that particular essence at that time. Sometimes I have been drawn to a particular plant, but have had to wait three years before the 'right' time to make that essence. When it eventually comes together, it can do so in a way that takes my breath away, and often I also realise that I would not have understood the teaching of that essence if I had tried to make it a year earlier.

I have sometimes been asked why I have created different essences from the same plant, such as in the case of Cyclamen, Yarrow or Comfrey. In my experience plants have some similarities with people. Each person can have a number of different abilities and interests. I could learn horse-riding from Eva, but also she could show me how to run my accounts programme, or how to bake really good Danish pastry, since these are some of her many talents or interests. Whatever she shows me it will have an 'Eva' flavour – reflecting her own unique energy and way of doing things.

So it is with flowers – each plant has quite a wide range of qualities that we can work with, but whatever essence we make from that plant, it will have an underlying theme that reflects the overall energy and qualities of that particular plant. If you look at the descriptions of

Yarrow essences made by different essence makers, you will notice some common threads running through all of their descriptions, which reflect the overall inspiration and energy of Yarrow.

I have thrown away a lot of the essences that I have made. As an essence maker, you know when it's a 'good' one, and when it's not (even if initially one is reluctant to admit it!). Sometimes I have made an essence and it has been 'good', but a year or so later I have re-made it, and the resulting essence has been far wider acting and profound, perhaps because I now have the understanding to realise its deeper implications, or maybe because the consciousness of the world has moved on, and me with it. Like many things that we do, the process of essence making is a continual journey of learning, and unfolding awareness – and I love it!

If you are interested in trying your hand at making some essences, you will find detailed information on how to make flower essences and how to interpret their qualities, in Chapters 3, 4 & 5 of: 'New Vibrational Flower Essences of Britain & Ireland' (see Suggested Reading List – at the back of this book)

Choosing and Using Essences

❊

If you have been working with this book and cards, and are interested in taking some flower essences, but feel unsure about how to go about choosing and using them, then hopefully this chapter will help you to understand the many different ways in which flower essences can be used.

Ready Prepared Combination Essences:
When first venturing into the world of flower essences, it can be helpful to first try some ready-made combination essences. There are many flower essence companies throughout the world, that produce ready to use, carefully blended, flower essence combinations. In the Useful Addresses section at the back of this book you will find some of these companies listed. You may also find ready-made flower essence blends on sale at your local health store.

Most people have come across the most commonly used rescue or crisis combinations, but you can now buy blends that cover issues such as poor self-confidence, grief, improving focus and concentration, motivational blends, blends for children, blends for animals, as well as wonderful blended flower essence mists (in atomiser bottles) for space clearing, as well as flower essence creams. All of these products give easy to follow directions for use, and can be used as and when you feel the need. Many people derive immense benefit and support from these carefully prepared blends.

Single Flower & Vibrational Essences:
If you are interested in working with the single essences described in this book, or in exploring other single essences from other ranges of

flower essences, either for yourself – or for your clients if you are a therapist – then read on!

Choosing flower essences – building a palette of essences:

Working with flower essences is a bit like being a painter. When we begin painting, we generally begin with a simple range of materials and a few colours, which we get to know, and then gradually add to these, as we discover new paints with new tones and colours. So it is when starting out with flower essences. We may begin by buying just a few essences that we feel that we can really relate to, and from there we may gradually build up a palette of essences.

Sensing the energy of different essence ranges:

Each essence maker's range of essences will have a particular overall quality or energy that we can sense if we read their literature, handle their essences, or work with their essences. Some essence ranges have a somewhat masculine energy, others can be very feminine – some relate to everyday issues and challenges, some are more esoteric – with a fine, high vibration, some relate to our inner child and to children, some are concerned with earth energy and shamanic ways of working. There are many different ranges of flower essences on sale now, both from Britain and from abroad.

Different people respond to different types of essences, at different times. As a therapist, I work with several different ranges of essences, including my own, so that I have a wide palette to suit the differing energies of my clients. Most flower essence therapists work in this way, and you will find that most flower essence makers have written in-depth handbooks for their particular range, which offer helpful insight into the qualities and uses of each of the single essences in their range.

To begin with, I would suggest that you visit a store that sells several different essence ranges, and books. Look at the essences, and take home some leaflets to read – or you can phone one of the mail-order companies to ask for literature to be sent to you – or do an internet search and check out some websites and download information on different essence ranges. It is very important to work with essences that you like the feel of, and that you as an individual are comfortable with. What suits one person will not necessarily suit another. We are generally more sensitive than we give ourselves credit for. It is important to follow your gut feelings and to choose from those essence ranges that really speak to you, rather than to just buy what other people rave about, or try to sell to you.

Choosing by use and knowledge of essence descriptions:

Once you have found one, two, or three essence ranges that really speak to you, then your best starting point is to look at an issue that you want to deal with in your life, or that you are facing at this current time. Next, try to see what the different aspects of this issue are, and whether there are any essences in the ranges that you are drawn to, that address these particular dynamics. If there are, then buy just these few essences, and work with them in combination for a while, and see how that goes. When a new issue arises, do the same again, and if appropriate, buy some further essences to work with.

To help identify the essences you might need, try to write some key-words that sum up the different feelings you have around an issue or situation that you want to address: angry, broken-hearted, rejected, lonely, resentful, guilty, fear of loss, fear of judgement, powerless, afraid of illness, fear of failure, apathetic, lacking in motivation, longing for approval, confused etc.

There is a Cross Reference Index of Mental, Emotional and Spiritual Categories, at the back of this book, with related essences. You can use this to help you to identify which essences most fit the dynamics of your issues. Most essence makers have excellent in-depth handbooks for the essences in their ranges, with a similar cross-reference section, to help you identify the most appropriate essences for yourself or for your clients. They also often run wonderful and very informative workshops on their particular essence ranges.

The Useful Addresses section at the back of the book lists those places that offer courses and workshops by British and international essence makers. If you are interested in working in-depth with a particular essence range, you will find attending one of these workshops will provide you with wonderful insight, and a much better understanding of the breadth, depth, and application of those essences.

If we limit ourselves initially to no more than three essence ranges, or better still, to just two ranges, them we can gradually build up an understanding of the individual essences in each range, and of just what their inspiration and uses might be. As new issues arise in our experience that we would like to address with flower essences, we can research new essences in these ranges, and buy additional essences, according to our needs.

Some therapists choose essences solely from their in-depth knowledge of the essences in their palette. This in-depth understanding is often built up over years of working on their own issues with essences, as well as from their work with clients.

Intuitive choosing, with dowsing, kinesiology, hand sensing or cards:

There are several ways in which people choose essences using intuitive methods. The advantage about an accurate intuitive use of dowsing, kinesiology or cards, is that it bypasses our 'little' mind, and our limited perception of what is going on, and will often reveal the real underlying dynamics and patterns that we need to address, that we might not have recognised with our everyday mind. Also, if we are an experienced dowser, or muscle tester, but are not familiar with the use of particular flower essences, then we have already an immediate and accurate way of choosing essences, that does not require an in-depth knowledge of the essences used.

I do not include details of how to dowse or how to muscle test in this book, because it is a subject that requires detailed information and is best learnt directly from an experienced practitioner – particularly muscle testing. However, in the Suggested Reading List, I have recommended an excellent book on dowsing that is written by master dowser and essence maker Arthur Bailey.

The important thing to remember if you are using an intuitive means of choosing, is to make sure that you are thoroughly centred before you use your method, that you are not trying to choose in a hurry, and that you preferably do so somewhere quiet, where you will not be disturbed. I also think that it is vital, if one is dowsing, muscle testing, or hand sensing over bottles of essences, that one cannot see the labels, or the names of the essences. In this way we are less likely to influence what is chosen. For this reason, the dowsing table at the back of the book only gives numbers for the essences, and not the names.

If you are experienced and confident with dowsing, then you can dowse with a pendulum for essences, either over the essences themselves in a shop (but this can be prove to be a distracting and rushed environment in which to choose), or over lists of essences. Be careful how you frame the question you are asking whilst you dowse. Don't just ask 'Which essences would be suitable for me?' or you may end up with half the shop and an empty wallet! Ask something more specific such as: 'Are there any essences from this range, that would help me (or my client), with this issue in this coming month?' For those familiar with using kinesiology/muscle testing, a similar approach is helpful.

Using flower essence cards:

Using flower essence cards is another very useful way of choosing essences for treatment for oneself or for clients. Again, the question one holds in one's mind, when picking the cards, should include in it that you are looking for essences that would be helpful to take at this particular time. If you wish to work with the essences in this book, then you can use any of the card spreads described, or any of your own, whilst holding the above principle in mind whilst choosing the cards. Some essence makers suggest spreading the cards out in front of us, face up, and then choosing those which most attract us, and those which most repel us, and putting these into two piles. We then go through each pile and narrow each pile down to four or five cards or less, and then work with these essences.

Hand sensing:

Many people have an ability to sense things with the palms of their hands or their fingertips. To do this they hold their fingers or their palms above a box of essences, and sense those essences that elicit a tingling, energetic feeling in the palm or fingers. In a way this is a form of hand dowsing or kinesiology. The same principles apply, as with the dowsing, cards and kinesiology – centreing, a quiet, undisturbed environment, specific questions, and hidden labels.

For a beginner, all of these abilities require practise. Not everyone can dowse, not everyone can muscle test or hand dowse. If we do find we have an ability with one of these methods, the more we practise, the better becomes our ability, and our accuracy.

Purchasing glass dropper bottles, brandy, vegetable glycerine and water

At the same time as you purchase your essences, you will need to buy some new clean, 25ml or 30ml, glass dropper bottles, a small bottle of spring water, and a small amount of brandy or vegetable glycerine (to act as a preservative in your dosage bottles), so that you will have all that you need in order to make up dosage bottles. Vegetable glycerine is used by those who can't tolerate, or who prefer not to use alcohol as a preservative. Glass dropper bottles can generally be bought either from your essence supplier, or from your local chemist. For larger quantities of dropper bottles, and for mail-order or local suppliers of vegetable glycerine, see the Useful Addresses section of this book.

What to do once you've bought some essences!

Stock Bottles:

If you have bought single essences, they will be what are known as 'stock' essences. This means that they are your stock bottles, from which you can make up further diluted treatment bottles. Your stock bottles, when stored carefully should have a shelf-life of at least ten years, (if you do not use them up before that time!).

Storage of essences:

Once you've bought your essences, please treat them with respect and keep them in a cool dark place, away from electrical equipment, microwaves, mobile phones, loud music or chaotic emotional energy. Some essence makers also prefer that their individual bottles of essences are stored not touching each other. Essence makers can often supply you with essence boxes with card dividers to prevent the essences from touching. (otherwise see Useful Addresses at the back of the book).

Most therapists keep their stock essences in a quiet cupboard or drawer, in a quiet room in the house. Don't carry them around in your handbag next to your mobile phone, or leave them on top of the microwave, t.v., computer or stereo. Equally, they don't appreciate being left to roast in your car on a hot summer's day, or being zapped too often by the x-ray machines at airports.

Taking essences direct from your stock bottles:
In emergencies, or when you feel that you don't need to make up a whole dosage bottle, for something that is a fleeting challenge, then you may wish to take just a few drops from a stock bottle, or from several bottles, onto your tongue, or onto the pulse points on your wrists, or into a glass of water or fruit juice. Whilst it is fine to take drops into your mouth, straight from your stock bottle, and will do you no harm, it is somewhat wasteful.

You should also ensure that if you do take drops directly from your stock bottles into your mouth, that you do not touch the pipette with your tongue, or with your fingers. In this way you will avoid bacterial contamination of your stock bottles. If you observe these simple measures, together with the suggestions given above for storage of essences, your stock bottles should keep their potency for many years.

Preparing a flower essence treatment for oneself or for clients:
Once you have chosen the essences that you feel most accurately relate to the issues that you or your client wish to address, you then have a choice as to how you work with those essences. Flower essences, being vibrational, can be used both internally and externally. Either way, they enter into our human energy field, and inspire our awareness.

Preparing Dosage Bottles:
The traditional, and most common way of taking flower essences, is to make up a dosage bottle.

You will need:
One clean 25ml or 30ml dropper bottle

Some spring water

A teaspoon of brandy, vodka or vegetable glycerine to act as a preservative

A self-adhesive label

To make up your bottle: add a teaspoon of your chosen preservative to the dropper bottle, then half fill the bottle with spring water (it helps to use a small jug for this). Now add your chosen essences. Most essence makers suggest how many drops of stock essences should be added to a dosage bottle. If you use muscle testing or dowsing, you can check how many drops using those methods, or you can use your intuition. Once you have added your chosen essences, then top up the bottle with spring water, screw on the dropper cap and label and date the bottle.

How many essences can you combine in a bottle?

How many different essences you combine in a bottle is really up to what feels most appropriate for you. Some people like to work with single essences, or with three or four at a time. Different things work for different people at different times. There are no hard and fast rules. In my experience, an appropriate number of essences to use in one treatment, can be any number between one and fourteen. More than that, and I would suggest that you might be creating rather a confusing mix of essences.

Some have suggested in the past that one shouldn't combine more than perhaps seven essences in one bottle, because of the confusion factor, but in recent years, quite complex combinations have been used by some therapists, when appropriate, and these have been found to be very effective. What seems important is not the number of essences in the bottle, but how accurately they relate to the often quite complex dynamics of an individual's situation.

Another factor in all of this, is that at this present time, we sometimes find ourselves facing several major issues in our lives, all at the once, and therefore our treatment needs to reflect that, in order to provide us with adequate support. This is especially so in the case of bereavement, where we can be faced with many powerful emotions and issues, as well as needing a lot of support, in order to cope with the demands of the situation. Therefore a dosage bottle can be quite complex, but this is not necessarily a bad thing, particularly if several of the essences included, are added to provide support and comfort.

How to use your dosage bottle:

You can take drops from your dosage bottle, straight onto your tongue, or you can add several drops from your dosage bottle to a glass of water or fruit juice, or to a sports bottle of water to sip throughout the day (this is particularly useful if you are out all day, or at work). If you are sensitive to alcohol, you can add several drops to a hot drink to allow the alcohol to evaporate before drinking.

How many drops you take is up to you, Some essence makers suggest how many drops you should use from a stock essence to make up a dosage bottle, and also how many drops to take from your dosage bottle – but in my experience I have found that it is best to follow one's own intuition, or to use dowsing or muscle testing to decide what most suits you or your client.

How often you take your essences is also up to you. Take them when you feel the need. If you are feeling very challenged, then have them with you throughout the day, or add some drops to a sports bottle so that you can take them when you need to. For a more long term issue, that is not so immediate or 'in your face', it is often easier to keep your bottle of drops beside your bed, and to just take some on waking, and some again before bed.

Some people like to add flower essences to their bath water, and you can try this by adding some drops from your dosage bottle to your bathwater. However, I wouldn't recommend this if your bottle is designed to be uplifting and energising, and you are wanting to take a bath to relax you before going to bed! (see further information in this chapter, on using essences in baths).

A quick fix sports bottle to help you through your day:
Sometimes we need to quickly put together some essences to help and support us with the challenges of the day ahead. We may not have time, or we may not need to make ourselves up a full dosage bottle. In this situation, we can just add some drops from a few selected stock essences, to a large sports bottle of water that we can carry about with us and drink throughout the day. This way we get to drink plenty of water (always a good thing!), as well as having an inconspicuous way of taking essences if we are at work, or out and about.

Using essences in atomisers:
Increasingly essences are being used in atomisers, to mist oneself, and

one's energy field, or to mist in the home or workplace. There are many wonderful flower essence space-clearing mists on the market, which have popularised this way of working with essences. Being vibrational, flower essences are absorbed equally well through the human energy field or the skin, as they are when they are taken orally. (For suppliers of atomisers, please see the Useful Addresses section at the back of this book).

Essences relating to crisis and trauma, and reassuring and settling essences can be added to atomisers used in accident and emergency rooms. Some schools have found it particularly helpful to use a blend of flower essences for focused attention, integration of understanding, and centred, calm interaction, in an atomiser used to mist classrooms, or their assembly hall. A similar blend of essences can be misted in offices, or the workplace. For the last two years, a primary school teacher I know, has used a relaxing and calming blend of essences to mist the bedrooms of children taken on an annual sports and adventure camp. She swears it works like a dream, and everyone settles down and goes to sleep, without any of the usual high spirits and shenanigans!

How to make up a flower essence atomiser bottle:

Most atomiser bottles come in 50ml or 100ml bottles, but sometimes one can get handbag-sized spritzers. Choose your essences, as described in the section on choosing essences, and add them to an atomiser filled with spring water. If you want the bottle to last for some time, you can add one fifth of the atomiser bottle's volume, of pure vodka, before nearly filling the atomiser with spring water. Add your essences to this bottle.

A few drops (between 5 & 10 drops) of essential oils can also be added to the bottle. Essential oils work synergistically with flower essences, when chosen to complement the purpose of the flower essence combination:- use rose oil to soothe and comfort; grapefruit and lemongrass to enliven and refresh; lavender to relax, and frankincense to centre and ground and purify. (Be warned! Some heavier essential oils can clog atomiser nozzles).

When you have made up your bottle, replace the atomiser cap, shake the bottle and mist the essences in your room, or into your aura or energy field. As with a dosage bottle of essences, how often you use your atomiser bottle depends on how often you feel the need to!

Atomisers for use with babies and toddlers:

You can make up atomisers of soothing flower essences, to mist gently around baby and toddler sleeping areas, or in rooms in which they spend most of their day. For very small babies, use just flower essences and pure spring water, without added vodka or essential oils. This is a very safe way of using flower essences with babies and toddlers.

Adding flower essences to cream or lotion bases or to massage oils:

Flower essences can also be added to creams, lotions or massage oils. For creams and lotions, you can either add flower essences to your everyday jar of face cream or moisturising lotion, or better still, you can buy a hypo-allergenic cream base or lotion, specifically to add flower essences to. (for suppliers of creams, lotions, jars and essential oils – see the Useful Addresses section at the back of this book).

Choose your flower essences as described above, then add them to a jar of hypo-allergenic lotion or cream, with essential oils as well, if you wish, (try 10-20 drops of essential oil per 50ml of lotion), and then stir until well combined using a clean lolly-stick, (available in packs from hardware stores or supermarkets). You can make up a crisis/rescue cream with appropriate flower essences for trauma/shock, together with flower essences to calm and reassure, mixed into a hypo-allergenic cream base, with added lavender essential oil – or you can try making a personal beauty lotion, with flower essences for loving and embracing yourself and your true beauty, plus your favourite sensual essential oils – such as rose or ylang ylang, added to a hypo-allergenic cream base.

When adding essences to massage oils, or to oils used for an aromatherapy treatment, choose essences that reflect the purpose of the massage or treatment – whether that massage or treatment is meant to energise, or to soothe, or to help with particular emotional issues. Add the essences to the oil/s and then stir or shake well before using. As with making up atomisers or creams, if you are adding essential oils, choose those which complement the energy and purpose of the flower essences chosen.

Adding flower essences to baths:

Flower essences can be added to baths, together with essential oils that complement the purpose of the essences (see suggestions above for which essential oils to use). It is very important to pre-mix just a few drops of essential oils into 50ml of carrier base oil, before adding a few drops of this blend to the bath. (Some essential oils can burn or irritate the skin if used undiluted in a bath). Use your intuition to decide how many drops of flower essences to add to your bath.

As I said earlier: some people like to add some drops from their current dosage bottle to their bathwater. However, I wouldn't recommend this if your bottle is designed to be uplifting and energising, and you are wanting to take a bath to relax you before going to bed!

Adding flower essences to baby and toddler baths, or to baths for those with sensitive skin:

For babies and toddlers, or those with sensitive skin, just add a few drops of appropriate and soothing flower essences to their bath water, and then stir well before bathing. Do not add essential oils as they are too strong for babies, toddlers and those with sensitive skins!

Using essences on pulse points:

Some people like to use essences on their pulse points instead of taking them orally. You can try putting a few drops of stock essences, or drops from your current dosage bottle, on the insides of your wrists. This area is one of the most commonly used 'pulse points', where many of our energy meridians meet. Putting drops of essences on these points allows the vibrational resonance of the essences to be quickly carried throughout much of our energy system.

If you are familiar with reflexology, acupuncture, healing, or other forms of body energy work you can experiment with different ways of using essences externally on the body's energy points.

A cautionary note on using flower essences externally:

Don't be lulled into thinking flower essences are so subtle that they can be used externally in a carefree fashion, without consideration and sensitivity. Flower essences can be very powerful when used externally, particularly when used on or over the chakra areas. Used in this way, they can sometimes prompt a rapid release of emotion or energy, and care should be taken, particularly when working with sensitive people. If in doubt, check carefully and thoroughly using dowsing or kinesiology, before using essences externally in your own, or your client's energy field. If you are at all concerned, stick to using essences internally.

How do flower essences work? How will I respond?

Flower essences work by vibration and resonance. It is as though they sing a pure note to us, and if we are a bit off-key, they show us how to come back in tune – what our true note is. In this sense they both inspire us with their truth and understanding, as well as point out to us where we are not 'singing true'. Often this happens in an alternating pattern, swinging between sometimes profound inspiration, and insight about how we may return to our centre and to a greater sense of wholeness and love – and then periods (often brief) of an intense awareness of exactly how we have created suffering for ourselves, and perhaps how painful that is, and how much we have had enough of doing so.

Some therapists call these periods 'an intensification of issues'. Their purpose seems to be one of helping us to become fully conscious and self-knowing, so that we no longer feel so tossed around by emotional waves, or patterns that we can't identify or understand how they arose. The more we come to know and understand ourselves, the more we can change and heal. If we find these periods of intensification too much, we can stop taking the essences for a bit, perhaps take some crisis/rescue combination, and then return to our original essences when we are ready for another go.

Perhaps that is the beauty of flower essences, in that they not only tell us the truth about life, ourselves and others, (a truth that is often far removed from our habitual way of perceiving things), but they also offer us at the same time a living experience of what it is like to be in that truth. It is as though, if we listen to that pure note long enough, we suddenly begin to experience the beauty of that and begin to vibrate with that resonance, instead of with our old note; until eventually we fully live that pure note. In this way we shift, and sometimes profoundly and joyously.

How often should I take essences? Does it get to be a habit?

Flower essences bear repeating! Often there are several layers and dynamics to a dissonant pattern or groove that we have got into, and these may have been reinforced by different situations over many years, or even lifetimes. Like peeling the layers of an onion, we may find ourselves revisiting the same dynamic repeatedly, but each time from a different angle, or at a deeper level of our understanding and awareness. We may find ourselves working with the same essence repeatedly over several years, and each time our understanding grows deeper and more profound.

Some people work through the layers and shift very fast, others like to go at a pace that suits them. There are no rules and no need to beat ourselves up if we think that we are being slow in 'getting it right'. Remember the parable in the Bible about the vineyard workers who came late, but who reaped the same reward as those who'd been there all day! The last shall be first, and the first shall be last – or perhaps, in modern terms – better late than never!

Children sometimes shift faster than adults, probably because they often have fewer imbedded and reinforced reactive patterns. However, this isn't always the case. In common with many other therapists I have seen many children who have come into this life with some very deep-rooted issues, which appear to have arisen from traumatic or challenging experiences in other lifetimes.

Many seem to be suffering from deep shock, trauma, or abandonment issues, which go far beyond the possible effects of their present birth, or gestational experience. Others seem to have come in with big, unresolved issues around power, abuse of power, power struggles and powerlessness. For many, the resolution of these issues appear to be their major long-term life challenge, and not something that is going to vanish overnight. Often there are shared issues and dynamics within the family, and it can be very helpful to work with an entire family, to begin to create a shift in understanding and awareness.

How far we go with flower essences is up to each of us as individuals. They can be used very gently and lightly, to calm, support and soothe, or they can be used to work on deep patterns and issues, and deeper and wider levels of awareness. The longer we work with flower essences, the more our conscious understanding changes, and the more we become aware that we are addressing fundamental perceptions and beliefs in the human psyche. Increasingly we come to realise the vastness and infinity of who we are and of all that is. In my understanding, that is the ultimate purpose of flower essences – to bring us to a full conscious realisation of who we are and of what Is.

Understanding, Forgiveness, & 'The Camp Fire Process'

❅

The 'Camp Fire Process' is included in this chapter with kind permission from Brandon Bays, who created this process in this particular form. (For further details of Brandon's books, tapes, courses etc, see Useful Addresses, at the back of this book).

The 'Camp Fire Process' is a process that I have found to be deeply healing and transformational on a number of occasions, and which I also recommend to clients. This process was put together by Brandon Bays as part of her transformational 'Journey' work, and can be found in her book 'The Journey'. It was originally designed to be used alongside her 'Emotional Journey' process and/or her 'Physical Journey' process. These three processes used together can bring profound healing and realisation to many deep emotional and physical issues in our lives.

However, it is also possible to use the 'Camp Fire Process' on it's own. I have used it many times myself, or have recommended clients to use it, for the following purposes:

- when we have never been able to forgive someone, or have never been able to understand why they behaved in the way that they did.

- when we are going through a painful and perhaps confusing time in a relationship and do not understand what is going on, or what the dynamics of the relationship are, or how to bring healing to that relationship (It helps us to understand what's really going on for us, and what's really going on with the other person/persons.).

- when we realise that we have had a particular issue, or experience with someone (it might be recently or a long time ago), and we have a lot of painful feelings arising from that experience which we have been unable to express.

- when we do not understand an aspect of ourselves and our behaviour, and we need to dialogue with that part of our being (inner child, critical parent etc) to understand why we behave or react in a certain way.

- when we uncover a painful earlier life experience, or past life experience, that relates to the patterns we have reproduced in our current life experience. We can use the 'Camp Fire Process' to dialogue with our former self, or with others involved in our past life situation.

What I find so healing about this process is that it really takes us away from seeing ourselves as the victim in a situation. It helps us to understand that nothing is ever done personally to us (even if it felt like that at the time). What we discover through this process, is the truth about what was really going on for each person in the story. We move from only seeing one side of the story (or perhaps only part of one side of the story) to really understanding what was going on for each person at the time.

What we often uncover is a shared issue – the strict, judgemental teacher may have inside her a rebellious child that she is trying hard to suppress. Faced with a rebellious child outside herself, she may project her own self-judgement and blame onto this child, because she reminds her so painfully of her own inner child that she judges so harshly and can't embrace. Situations and experiences in relationships can often be very confusing. The wonder of the 'Camp Fire Process' is that we can finally see and really understand with clarity the dynamics between people. With real understanding can come a sudden letting go of judgement, and a wonderful release of a shared pattern or dynamic that may have held both parties back.

I once used the 'Camp Fire Process' to deal with a very painful shared issue that I had with a friend. This friend had recently died following a brief illness, and I had found myself at her memorial service, feeling acutely aware of our 'unfinished business' and of a painful misunderstanding of each other that we had never managed to clear.

When I did the 'Camp Fire Process' and she came (in spirit) to the Camp Fire to talk about this, I finally realised that we both shared the same issue around the pain of rejection, but that it had been masked by our different ways of reacting to situations.

The complete letting go of judgement and the love that flowed between us as a result of this understanding, was overwhelming and wonderfully healing after so many years of pain and misunderstanding. It was as though we had set each other free from the cages that we had put each other in. The love that she brought to the process, and the eagerness that she expressed at a soul level to clear this misunderstanding, brought so much light and joy to this understanding.

When I first became involved with spiritual healing 21 years ago, I was introduced to a similar process, in which one spoke across an imaginary candle flame in the same way to another person, or to their soul, in the presence of each person's higher self and guides (mentors). However, Brandon has refined this process until it has become a much deeper and more profound experience.

In order to follow 'Camp Fire Process' successfully, so that you experience it's full potential for healing, you need to be aware of the following points:

- You need to be able to take as long as the process takes. It can't be rushed. (I would suggest a minimum of an hour, and preferably to allow for up to two hours).

- You need to be in a space where you will be undisturbed and where you will feel uninhibited about speaking aloud, or crying.

- You **do need** to speak out loud all your feelings and all your questions. In my experience, it is very important to actually give voice to these feelings. Many of us have a block or resistance between our heart and throat chakras because of all the feelings that we have stuffed down over the years, or over lifetimes. When voiced out loud, this process can help to release these blocks.

- It is also important to take as long as you need to say everything that you need to say. Sometimes in this process, we say so much, and yet it's not all cleared – there's still some residue of anger or pain. If we sit with the feelings around that for a while, we will generally uncover whatever else we need to say, or further questions that we need to ask until we are completely empty and until we have completely understood what was going on.

- If you realise that you are not wholly ready to let go judgement and anger and forgive, then there is more to say or more questions to ask. Be patient with yourself – understanding will come. Sometimes asking the mentor the question 'What would have to happen in order to forgive?' will bring insight into what is needed in order to let go of these feelings.

- Some people like to go through a process such as this on their own. If this is you, then read through the 'Camp Fire' instructions several times, to memorise it, and maybe write yourself some prompt notes or keywords to check as you are going through the process – or read the instructions onto a tape, that you can then pause at the bits you where you need to carry out that particular instruction. Brandon Bays also sells guided tapes containing all of the 'Journey' processes (these are available from her website, or through bookshops – see Useful Addresses.)

- Some people like to have a friend, or a therapist guide them through this process. You can either get a friend, or a therapist you know, to read you the script, or you can go to someone in your area specifically trained in 'Journey' work.

- In following the instructions below, remember that you can dialogue with just one person, or with an aspect of yourself, or one by one with several people involved in a situation. Adapt the wording of the instructions to suit whichever you are doing.

'The Camp Fire Process' instructions

Read slowly and carefully. Whenever you see ...... pause and give your partner (or yourself) sufficient time to fully experience the answer to the questions.

Imagine a camp fire ...... the nature of which is eternal silence, unconditional love. Imagine a **younger you** sitting at this fire ......

Now picture the **present you** sitting at the fire ...... Also at this fire is a **mentor** whose divine wisdom you trust – it can be someone you know or would like to know, a saint, a sage, or someone born of your imagination; someone in whose presence you feel safe ...... Now bring to the fire the specific people who are involved with your issue ...... who else needs to be at this camp fire? ...... *(let answer).*

Can you see the camp fire? ...... Can you see the **younger you?** ...... The **present you?** ...... The **mentor?** ...... Who else is there? ...... *(let them answer – write down the names so you can refer to them specifically, i.e. Mother, Father, Loved One etc.)* Of the people involved with your issue, ask the **younger you** to which ONE or TWO would you like to speak? ...... *(If two people, ask: To whom would you like to speak first? ......)*

<u>Go through **all** the following questions (1 – 11) for **each** person spoken to.</u>

1. Everyone is now sitting in the protective presence of this fire of unconditional love and acceptance. The **younger you** may have experienced a great deal of pain in the past. Let the **younger you** speak now from that previous pain, saying what needs to be said, and letting —— *(Mother, Father, Loved One etc.)* hear what needs to be heard ...... *(long pause)*

2. Knowing that —— *(Mother, Father, Loved One etc.)* was probably doing the best he/she could with the resources he/she had at the time, let him/her reply ...... *(pause for reply).*

3. What does the **younger you** have to reply to that? ...... *(let answer).*

4. If —— *(Mother, Father, Loved One etc.)* were to reply, not from the level of the personality, but from the level of the soul, what might he/she say? ...... *(let answer).*

5. How does the **younger you** have to reply to that? ...... *(continue until empty).*

6. Does the **mentor** have anything to add? ...... *(let answer).*

7. What does the **present you** have to say to —— *(Mother, Father, Loved One etc.)?* ...... *(continue until empty).*

8. What would —— *(Mother, Father, Loved One etc.)* reply from the level of the soul? ...... *(let answer).*

9. Does anyone have anything more to add? ...... *(continue conversation until empty).*

10. When the **younger you** is ready, ask: 'Even though his/her behaviour may not have been acceptable by **any** standards, and even if you in no way condone his/her behaviour, are you willing to **completely and utterly** forgive him/her from the bottom of your heart?' ...... *(let answer).* Now go ahead and forgive him/her ...... *(let forgive).*

11. When the **present you** is ready, ask 'Even though his/her behaviour may not have been acceptable by **any** standards, and even if you in no way condone his/her behaviour, are you willing to **completely and utterly** forgive him/her from the bottom of your heart?' ...... *(wait for answer).* Now go ahead and forgive him/her ...... *(let forgive).*

If you have anyone else involved in this situation that you need to speak to, repeat the process of questions 1 to 11, with each person, so that all is said and heard. When you have completed your process, continue by saying the following:

Say: Go ahead and forgive them all, sending them your blessings. Allow them to merge into the fire which is the source of all life ...... Then turn to the **younger you** and say 'I promise you will **never** have to experience this previous pain again. I forgive you for any pain which was caused, because you didn't have access to the resources that I do now, and I promise you can have access to them any time you like. I love you and will always protect you' ...... Then hugging the **younger you,** let yourself merge, allowing the **younger you** to grow up with this forgiveness inside ...... Turning to the **mentor,** thank him/her ...... Now come back to the present.

Cross Reference Index of Issues

(Combination essences are indicated in italics)

Abandonment: Wild Cyclamen, Red Deadnettle, Father Sun, Heart Mother, Grandmothers Arms, Sweet Pea, *Healing Grief (comb)*

Abundance/Prosperity: Living the Dream, Orange Wallflower, Pussy Willow, Heart Mother, Golden Blessings, Celandine, *Infinite Abundance (comb)*

Abuse Issues: Inner Fire, Red Poppy, Goldenrod, Physostegia, Red Gladiolus, Horse Chestnut Leaf Bud, Blue Delphinium, Original Innocence, Phoenix Rebirth, Crab Apple Fruit, *Self Worth (comb)*, *Sexual Healing (comb)*, *Forgiveness (comb)*

Acceptance/Embrace: Comfrey, Sweet Hunza, Loving Me – Loving You, Yellow Hyacinth, Beauty in the Eye, Phoenix Rebirth, Original Innocence, Crab Apple Fruit, Red Quince, *Forgiveness (comb)*

Addictive Behaviour: Heart Mother, Disciple of the Heart, With Love, Original Innocence, Red Poppy, Comfrey, Cyclamen, Pussy Willow, Crab Apple Fruit, Loving Me – Loving You

Adolescence: Goldenrod, Physostegia, Red Quince, Blue Delphinium, Wild Cyclamen, Father Sun, Heart Mother, Red Poppy, The Rose, Passionate Life, Disciple of the Heart, *Self Worth (comb)*

Aging: Sky Blue Comfrey, Divine Being, Crab Apple Fruit, Speedwell, Loving Me – Loving You, *True Beauty (comb)*

Aloofness: Pink Cherry, Yellow Hyacinth, Beauty in the Eye, Loving Me – Loving You, Orange Wallflower, True Power, Original Innocence, Red Deadnettle, One Being, Child's Play, Reunion

Anger/Frustration/Bitterness/Resentment: Inner Fire, Red Poppy, Pussy Willow, Goldenrod, Red Deadnettle, Red Quince, Phoenix Rebirth, Blue Delphinium, Blue Salvia, Honesty, *Forgiveness (comb), Self Worth (comb)*

Apathy: Red Poppy, Green Alexanders, With Love, Passionate Life, Disciple of the Heart, Golden Blessings, Living The Dream, Celandine, Sweet Hunza, Comfrey, *Passionate Life (comb)*

Attention/Focus: Speedwell, Lilac, With Love, Reunion, Blue Salvia, Physostegia, *Working Harmony (comb)*

Authority issues/conflicts: Goldenrod, At the Heart of Being, Wild Cyclamen, Physostegia, Blue Delphinium, Red Poppy, Inner Fire, True Power, Disciple of the Heart, Red Quince, *Self Worth (comb), Working Harmony (comb), Forgiveness (comb)*

Avoidance: Disciple of the Heart, With Love, Speedwell, Lilac, Comfrey, Red Poppy, Passionate Life, Beauty in the Eye, *Working Harmony (comb), Self Worth (comb)*

Balance: Reunion, Cherry Plum Fruit, Speedwell, *Peace in a Storm (comb), Working Harmony (comb) Women's Balance (comb)*

Base Chakra: Stitchwort, Red Clover, Divine Being, Letting Go, Inner Fire, Red Poppy, Passionate Life

Beauty: Loving Me – Loving You, Beauty in the Eye, Honesty, Original Innocence, Yellow Hyacinth, Pink Cherry, Crab Apple Fruit, *True Beauty (comb)*

Blame: Red Poppy, Red Quince, Red Deadnettle, Phoenix Rebirth, Yellow Hyacinth, Pink Cherry, Original Innocence, *Forgiveness (comb)*

Body Image: Crab Apple Fruit, Loving Me – Loving You, Honesty, Divine Being, Green Alexanders, Stitchwort, *True Beauty (comb), Self Healing (comb), Self Worth (comb)*

Bonding: Pink Cherry, Beauty in the Eye, Yellow Hyacinth, Father Sun, Heart Mother, Grandmothers Arms

Boundaries: Physostegia, Peaceful Detachment, Goldenrod, Red Poppy, Inner Fire, Blue Delphinium, Violet, Divine Being, Heart Flow, *Light Heart Space (comb), Self Worth (comb)*

Breakdown: Cherry Plum Fruit, Cyclamen, Speedwell, Original Innocence, At the Heart of Being, Red Poppy, Crimean Snowdrop, Phoenix Rebirth, Sweet Hunza, Lilac, Reunion, Pussy Willow, With Love, *Peace in a Storm (comb), Forgiveness (comb)*

Brokenheartedness: Red Deadnettle, Red Quince, Heart Flow, Pure Love, Letting Go, Crimean Snowdrop, Sweet Hunza, *Forgiveness (comb), Healing Grief (comb)*

Bullying: Goldenrod, Red Poppy, Physostegia, Blue Delphinium, Inner Fire, True Power, Yellow Hyacinth, *Self-Worth (comb), Working Harmony (comb)*

Calm: Red Clover, Speedwell, Bluebell Grove, Lilac, At the Heart of Being, Cherry Plum Fruit, Peaceful Detachment, Divine Being, One Being, Sky Blue Comfrey, Comfrey, Stitchwort, Letting Go, Crimean Snowdrop, *Peace in a Storm (comb), Sleep Well (comb)*

Catharsis: Cherry Plum Fruit, Heart Flow, Physostegia, Crimean Snowdrop, Red Clover, Letting Go, Peaceful Detachment, Sweet Hunza, Honesty, Red Quince, *Peace in a Storm (comb), Healing Grief (comb)*

Centering: Cherry Plum Fruit, Red Clover, Comfrey, At the Heart of Being, Goldenrod, Wild Cyclamen, One Being, Physostegia, Lilac, Speedwell, *Peace in a Storm (comb), Working Harmony (comb)*

Change: Letting Go, Pussy Willow, Passionate Life, Reunion, Red Poppy, Father Sun, Goldenrod, Wild Cyclamen, Sweet Pea, Living the Dream, *Passionate Life (comb), Peace in a Storm (comb)*

Child and Parent: Heart Mother, Pink Cherry, Father Sun, Goldenrod, Wild Cyclamen, Grandmothers Arms, Original Innocence, Child's Play, *Take Time (comb)*

Cleansing: Crab Apple Fruit, Original Innocence, Crimean Snowdrop, Peaceful Detachment, *Lighter Space (comb)*

Clairvoyance/Clairaudience: Blue Salvia, One Being, Speedwell, Reunion, Pussy Willow, Blue Delphinium, Rosebay Willowherb, *At One (comb)*

Clarity: Blue Salvia, Speedwell, Goldenrod, Physostegia, One Being, At the Heart of Being, Blue Delphinium, Inner Fire, Lilac, Pussy Willow, *At One (comb), Self Worth (comb)*

Co-Dependency: Pure Love, Goldenrod, Father Sun, Heart Mother, Loving Me – Loving You, Honesty, At the Heart of Being, Wild Cyclamen, Physostegia, Blue Delphinium, Red Deadnettle, Stitchwort, Red Deadnettle, Orange Wallflower, *Sexual Healing (comb), Self Worth (comb)*

Communication: Blue Delphinium, Honesty, The Rose, Celandine, Red Quince, Blue Salvia, Heart Flow, *Self Expression (comb)*

Compassion: Pink Cherry, Yellow Hyacinth, Phoenix Rebirth, Red Quince, Original Innocence, *Forgiveness (comb)*

Connection to Spirit: One Being, At the Heart of Being, Sweet Pea, Reunion, Rosebay Willowherb, *At One (comb)*

Connection to Nature and the Spirit in Nature: Green Alexanders, Rosebay Willowherb, Heart Mother, Grandmothers Arms, Bluebell Grove, Stitchwort, *At One (comb)*

Confidence: Goldenrod, Physostegia, Blue Delphinium, Honesty, Wild Cyclamen, Red Quince, At the Heart of Being, Loving Me – Loving You, Red Poppy, Inner Fire, True Power, Violet, Yellow Hyacinth, Father Sun, The Rose, Passionate Life, Green Alexanders, Divine Being, Blue Salvia, *Self-Worth (comb)*

Conflict Resolution: True Power, Red Quince, Phoenix Rebirth, Blue Delphinium, Physostegia, Goldenrod, Yellow Hyacinth, Red Poppy, Blue Salvia, Inner Fire, *Forgiveness (comb)*

Confusion/Indecision: Blue Salvia, Inner Fire, Lilac, Reunion, With Love, Disciple of the Heart, Beauty in the Eye, Blue Delphinium, Physostegia, Speedwell, Goldenrod, At the Heart of Being, *Working Harmony (comb), Self Worth (comb)*

Courage: Passionate Life, Red Clover, Letting Go, Stitchwort, Blue Delphinium, Honesty, Goldenrod, Inner Fire, Physostegia, Living the Dream, Passionate Life, Cherry Plum Fruit, Divine Being, Crimean Snowdrop, *Peace in a Storm (comb), Passionate Life (comb)*

Creativity: Cyclamen, Pussy Willow, Comfrey, Lilac, Reunion, Speedwell, Celandine, The Rose, Blue Delphinium, Living the Dream, Child's Play, *Make Time (comb), Self Expression (comb)*

Crisis: Cherry Plum Fruit, Red Clover, Peaceful Detachment, Sweet Hunza, Crimean Snowdrop, Physostegia, Stitchwort, Speedwell, Letting Go, Comfrey, Sweet Pea, Divine Being, *Peace in a Storm (comb)*

Criticism: Pink Cherry, Yellow Hyacinth, Beauty in the Eye, Loving Me – Loving You, Celandine, Red Quince, Original Innocence, Crab Apple Fruit

Crystal Clearing: Original Innocence, *Lighter Space (comb)*

Cutting Ties: Peaceful Detachment, Heart Mother, Letting Go, Inner Fire, *Light Heart Space (comb)*

Cynicism: Celandine, Pink Cherry, Yellow Hyacinth, Beauty in the Eye, Blue Salvia, Reunion, Child's Play, One Being, Living the Dream

Daydreaming/Inattention: Speedwell, Disciple of the Heart, With Love, Stitchwort, Reunion, Lilac, *Working Harmony (comb)*

Death, Dying: Letting Go, Sky Blue Comfrey, Sweet Pea, Cherry Plum Fruit, Divine Being, Stitchwort, Red Clover, At the Heart of Being, *Peace in a Storm (comb)*

Defensiveness: Red Quince, Heart Flow, Yellow Hyacinth, Red Deadnettle, Orange Wallflower, Red Poppy, Pure Love, Pink Cherry, Phoenix Rebirth, Divine Being, Original Innocence, Crab Apple Fruit, *Self Worth (comb), Forgiveness (comb)*

Denial: Honesty, Blue Salvia, Blue Delphinium, Original Innocence, Cherry Plum Fruit, Beauty in the Eye, Yellow Hyacinth, Celandine, Golden Blessings, *Self Worth (comb)*

Despair: Sweet Hunza, Wild Cyclamen, Red Poppy, Divine Being, Comfrey, *Peace in a Storm (comb)*

Detachment: Peaceful Detachment, Crimean Snowdrop, Red Clover, Heart Mother, Divine Being, Letting Go, *Light Heart Space (comb)*

Discernment: Blue Salvia, Physostegia, Goldenrod, One Being, Inner Fire, Red Quince,

Discipline/Self-Discipline: Disciple of the Heart, With Love, Lilac, Speedwell, Pussy Willow, Living the Dream, *Working Harmony (comb)*

Dissatisfaction: Beauty in the Eye, Comfrey, Yellow Hyacinth, Golden Blessings, Celandine, Passionate Life, Living the Dream, Red Poppy, Cyclamen, Goldenrod, Blue Delphinium, Passionate Life (comb), *Infinite Abundance (comb)*

Doubt: Blue Salvia, Goldenrod, Inner Fire, Living the Dream, One Being, Red Poppy, Sweet Pea, Pussy Willow, *Self Worth (comb)*

Earth Connection: Heart Mother, Grandmothers Arms, Stitchwort, Rosebay Willowherb, One Being, Green Alexanders, Comfrey

Energy: Red Poppy, Passionate Life, Green Alexanders, With Love, Pussy Willow, Inner Fire, Disciple of the Heart, Cyclamen, Heart Mother *Time Out (comb), Self Healing (comb), Passionate Life (comb)*

Enthusiasm: Passionate Life, Red Poppy, Living the Dream, Disciple of the Heart, With Love, Child's Play, Green Alexanders, Comfrey, Celandine, *Passionate Life (comb)*

Exhaustion: Red Poppy, Cyclamen, Pussy Willow, Speedwell, Bluebell Grove, With Love, Green Alexanders, Stitchwort, Heart Mother, Grandmothers Arms, Living the Dream, *Sleep Well (comb), Time Out (comb)*

Faith: Living the Dream, Sweet Pea, Pussy Willow, With Love, Divine Being Peaceful Detachment, Red Clover, Lilac, Speedwell, Red Poppy, *Peace in a Storm (comb), Infinite Abundance (comb)*

Fathering: Father Sun, Goldenrod, Physostegia, At the Heart of Being, Wild Cyclamen, True Power, Red Poppy, Blue Delphinium, Inner Fire, Passionate Life, *Self Worth (comb)*

Fear of Illness: Divine Being, Stitchwort, Red Clover, Crimean Snowdrop, Letting Go, Crab Apple Fruit, Sweet Hunza, *Self Healing (comb), Peace in a Storm (comb)*

Fear of Failure: Red Poppy, Passionate Life, Goldenrod, Inner Fire, Father Sun, Wild Cyclamen, Lilac, Speedwell, The Rose, *Passionate Life (comb), Self Worth (Comb), Self Expression (comb)*

Fear of Lack: Living the Dream, Orange Wallflower, Pussy Willow, Heart Mother, Golden Blessings, Celandine, Red Poppy, The Rose, Pure Love, *Infinite Abundance (comb)*

Fear of Speaking Out: Blue Delphinium, Physostegia, Goldenrod, Red Poppy, Honesty, At the Heart of Being, Loving Me – Loving You, Violet, True Power, Red Quince, Red Deadnettle, Heart Flow, *Self Expression (comb)*

Feminine Energy: Pink Cherry, Pussy Willow, Cyclamen, Heart Mother, Grandmothers Arms, Loving Me – Loving You, With Love, Disciple of the Heart, Speedwell, *Take Time (comb)*

Flexibility: Pussy Willow, Disciple of the Heart, Lilac, Speedwell, Living the Dream, With Love, Yellow Hyacinth, Comfrey, *Working Harmony (comb), Take Time (comb)*

Forgiveness: Phoenix Rebirth, Original Innocence, Blue Delphinium, Pink Cherry, Yellow Hyacinth, Red Quince, Red Deadnettle, Poppy, Inner Fire, *Forgiveness (comb)*

Frustration/Frustrated Energy: Red Poppy, Inner Fire, Blue Salvia, Yellow Hyacinth, Blue Delphinium, Goldenrod, True Power, Wild Cyclamen, Comfrey, Sweet Hunza, Living the Dream, *Self Worth (comb)*

Gratitude: Golden Blessings, Celandine, Beauty in the Eye, *Infinite Abundance (comb)*

Grief: Letting Go, Cherry Plum Fruit, Heart Flow, Father Sun, Sweet Pea, Red Deadnettle, Cyclamen, Wild Cyclamen, Grandmothers Arms, Heart Mother, Pink Cherry, Crimean Snowdrop, Passionate Life, *Healing Grief (comb), Peace in a Storm (comb)*

Grounding: Red Poppy, Comfrey, Speedwell, Cherry Plum Fruit, Disciple of the Heart, Goldenrod, Physostegia, Heart Mother, Grandmothers Arms, Lilac, Wild Cyclamen, At the Heart of Being, Father Sun, Stitchwort, *Peace in a Storm (comb), Self-Worth (comb)*

Group Work: Physostegia, Red Quince, Blue Delphinium, Goldenrod, Disciple of the Heart, Lilac, Speedwell, Phoenix Rebirth, Loving Me – Loving You, Pussy Willow, One Being, *Working Harmony (comb)*

Guilt: Original Innocence, Crab Apple Fruit, Heart Flow, Loving Me – Loving You, Yellow Hyacinth, Red Quince, Disciple of the Heart, Pink Cherry, *Forgiveness (comb)*

Guidance: Goldenrod, At the Heart of Being, Blue Salvia, One Being, Speedwell, Sweet Pea, Physostegia, Cyclamen, Wild Cyclamen, Lilac, Pussy Willow, *At One (comb)*

Heart Chakra: Pink Cherry, Heart Flow, Yellow Hyacinth, Grandmothers Arms, Heart Mother, Pure Love, Loving Me – Loving You, Cyclamen, Pussy Willow, Wild Cyclamen, Red Clover, Speedwell, Red Quince, *Forgiveness (comb), Take Time (comb)*

Honesty: Honesty, Loving Me – Loving You, Heart Flow, Blue Delphinium, Cherry Plum Fruit, Original Innocence, Red Quince, *Self Worth (comb)*

Hyperactivity: Speedwell, Bluebell Grove, Cherry Plum Fruit, Goldenrod, Original Innocence, Reunion, Disciple of the Heart, *Sleep Well (comb), Working Harmony (comb)*

Imagination: Child's Play, Reunion, Cyclamen, Living the Dream

Impatience: Speedwell, Comfrey, Pussy Willow, Pink Cherry, Lilac, Yellow Hyacinth, Grandmothers Arms, Red Poppy, Loving Me – Loving You, Sweet Hunza, *Take Time (comb), Working Harmony (comb)*

Incarnation Choices: Stitchwort, The Rose, At the Heart of Being, True Power, Living the Dream, Divine Being, With Love

Indecision: Reunion, Blue Salvia, Inner Fire, Lilac, With Love, Disciple of the Heart, Beauty in the Eye, Blue Delphinium, Physostegia, Speedwell, Goldenrod, One Being, At the Heart of Being, True Power, Living the Dream

Independence: Wild Cyclamen, Father Sun, Goldenrod, Physostegia, Red Poppy, Blue Delphinium, Inner Fire, Pure Love, Heart Mother, *Self Worth (comb)*

Inner Child: Heart Mother, Father Sun, Pink Cherry, Grandmother's Arms, Wild Cyclamen, Goldenrod, Orange Wallflower, Red Quince, *Take Time (comb), Self Worth (comb)*

Insensitivity: Pink Cherry, Yellow Hyacinth, Speedwell, Beauty in the Eye, Pussy Willow, Reunion

Integration: Reunion, At the Heart of Being, Lilac, Speedwell, One Being, The Rose, Cherry Plum Fruit, Pussy Willow, *Working Harmony (comb)*

Integrity: Goldenrod, At the Heart of Being, Physostegia, Peaceful Detachment, Heart Mother, Disciple of the Heart, Blue Delphinium, True Power, Violet, Inner Fire, Red Poppy, Phoenix Rebirth, Wild Cyclamen, *Self Worth (comb), Working Harmony (comb), Light Heart Space (comb)*

Intimacy: Pink Cherry, Loving Me – Loving You, Honesty, Heart Flow, Pure Love, Original Innocence, Yellow Hyacinth, Beauty in the Eye, Red Gladiolus, Horse Chestnut Leaf Bud, Pussy Willow, Speedwell, *Make Love (comb), Sexual Healing (comb)*

Intuition: Blue Salvia, One Being, Goldenrod, Pussy Willow, At the Heart of Being, Lilac, Wild Cyclamen, Speedwell, *At One (comb)*

Jealousy/Envy: True Power, Red Poppy, Red Deadnettle, Red Quince, Violet, Goldenrod, Original Innocence, Loving Me – Loving You, Golden Blesssings, Celandine

Joy: Celandine, Golden Blessings, Child's Play, Living the Dream

Judgement: Beauty in the Eye, Yellow Hyacinth, Goldenrod, Physostegia, Red Deadnettle, Red Quince, Phoenix Rebirth, Original Innocence, Crab Apple Fruit, Loving Me – Loving You, *Forgiveness (comb), Self Worth (comb)*

Life Purpose/Direction: Disciple of the Heart, Cyclamen, Wild Cyclamen, Father Sun, Goldenrod, Red Poppy, With Love, Passionate Life, The Rose, Violet, Stitchwort, Goldenrod, At the Heart of Being, *Passionate Life (comb), Self Worth (comb), Self Expression (comb)*

Listening: Blue Delphinium, Red Quince, Goldenrod, Pussy Willow, Grandmothers Arms, Physostegia, Cherry Plum Fruit, Yellow Hyacinth, At the Heart of Being, *Working Harmony (comb)*

Love/Self-love/Acceptance: Pure Love, Pink Cherry, Loving Me-Loving You, Orange Wallflower, Yellow Hyacinth, Beauty in the Eye, Honesty, Heart Flow, Cyclamen, Heart Mother, Grandmothers Arms, Crab Apple Fruit, Original Innocence, At the Heart of Being, Cherry Plum Fruit, Sweet Pea, *True Beauty (comb), Forgiveness (comb)*

Loneliness/Isolation: Orange Wallflower, Wild Cyclamen, Sweet Pea, At the Heart of Being, Blue Salvia, One Being, Pure Love

Longing: Pure Love, Heart Mother, Orange Wallflower, Goldenrod, Father Sun, Golden Blessings, Beauty in the Eye

Masculine Energy: Horse Chestnut Leaf Bud, Father Sun, Goldenrod, Red Poppy, Inner Fire, Physostegia, At the Heart of Being, Passionate Life, *Self Worth (comb), Passionate Life (comb)*

Meditation: One Being, At the Heart of Being, Reunion, Speedwell, Comfrey, Bluebell Grove, *At One (comb)*

Men's Sexuality: Horse Chestnut Leaf Bud, Father Sun, Goldenrod, Red Poppy, Inner Fire, Physostegia, Passionate Life, Red Gladiolus, Pure Love, Loving Me – Loving You, Pink Cherry, Speedwell, Yellow Hyacinth, Beauty in the Eye, *Sexual Healing (comb), Make Love (comb)*

Mental Focus/Learning/Memory: Speedwell, Comfrey, Lilac, Blue Salvia, Reunion, Disciple of the Heart, Red Poppy, Pussy Willow, *Working Harmony (comb)*

Mothering: Pink Cherry, Heart Mother, Cyclamen, Grandmothers Arms, Pussy Willow, Wild Cyclamen, *Take Time (comb), Women's Balance (comb)*

Motivation: Red Poppy, Passionate Life, Disciple of the Heart, With Love, Cyclamen, Goldenrod, Heart Mother, Father Sun, The Rose, Stitchwort , *Passionate Life (comb), Self Worth (comb)*

Neediness: Orange Wallflower, Father Sun, Heart Mother, Pure Love, Wild Cyclamen, Goldenrod, Grandmothers Arms, Pink Cherry, Loving Me – Loving You, Honesty, Red Deadnettle, Violet

Panic: Red Clover, Divine Being, Cherry Plum Fruit, Letting Go, Crimean Snowdrop, Stitchwort, *Peace in a Storm (comb), Self Healing (comb)*

Patience: Comfrey, Speedwell, Pussy Willow, Pink Cherry, Cyclamen, Yellow Hyacinth, Grandmothers Arms, Loving Me – Loving You, Living the Dream, Sweet Hunza, *Take Time (comb), Working Harmony (comb)*

Pessimism: Celandine, Golden Blessings, Living the Dream, Yellow Hyacinth, Red Poppy, Lilac, Speedwell, Passionate Life, Wild Cyclamen, *Infinite Abundance (comb), Passionate Life (comb)*

Phobias: Letting Go, Red Clover, Crimean Snowdrop, Crab Apple Fruit, Divine Being, Passionate Life, Green Alexanders, *Peace in a Storm (comb), Passionate Life (comb), Self Healing (comb)*

Play/Fun: Child's Play, Passionate Life, Reunion, Original Innocence, *Take Time (comb), Passionate Life (comb)*

Power/Powerlessness: True Power, Goldenrod, Inner Fire, Red Poppy, Physostegia, Blue Delphinium, Divine Being, At the Heart of Being, Red Clover, Living the Dream, Sweet Hunza, Wild Cyclamen, *Self Worth (comb)*

Prejudice: Yellow Hyacinth, Beauty in the Eye, Goldenrod, Pink Cherry, Original Innocence, Crab Apple Fruit, Loving Me-Loving You, *Forgiveness (comb)*

Pride: Goldenrod, True Power, Pink Cherry, Honesty, Loving Me – Loving You, Red Quince, Original Innocence, Yellow Hyacinth, Violet, Blue Delphinium, Beauty in the Eye, Self Worth (comb)

Procrastination: Disciple of the Heart, With Love, Lilac, Speedwell, Pussy Willow, Wild Cyclamen, Blue Delphinium, Goldenrod, Red Poppy, Inner Fire, Passionate Life, Violet, True Power, The Rose, Stitchwort, Green Alexanders, *Passionate Life (comb)*, *Self Worth (comb)*, *Self Expression (comb)*, *Working Harmony (comb)*

Protection: Divine Being, Peaceful Detachment, Physostegia, Red Clover, Red Poppy, Inner Fire, Crimean Snowdrop, Red Quince, Heart *Mother*, *Light Heart Space (comb)*, *Lighter Space (comb)*

Rebelliousness: Goldenrod, True Power, Original Innocence, Physostegia, Disciple of the Heart, Blue Delphinium, Wild Cyclamen, Red Quince, Blue Delphinium, Red Poppy, *Self Worth (comb)*

Rejection: Red Deadnettle, Wild Cyclamen, Red Quince, Red Poppy, Goldenrod, Loving Me – Loving You, Original Innocence, Orange Wallflower, Heart Flow, Phoenix Rebirth, *Forgiveness (comb)*, *Healing Grief (comb)*, *Passionate Life (comb)*

Relationships: Pure Love, Orange Wallflower, Loving Me – Loving You, Yellow Hyacinth, Beauty in the Eye, Blue Delphinium, Pink Cherry, Goldenrod, Honesty, Heart Flow, Father Sun, Heart Mother, Red Quince, Red Deadnettle, Physostegia, Red Poppy, Inner Fire, Wild Cyclamen, Red Gladiolus, Horse Chestnut Leaf Bud, *Self Worth (comb)*, *Sexual Healing (comb)*

Relaxation: Bluebell Grove, Cyclamen, Speedwell, Lilac, Red Clover, Heart Mother, Child's Play, Speedwell, With Love, Grandmothers Arms, Pussy Willow, Letting Go, Stitchwort, *Time Out (comb)*, *Sleep Well (comb)*

Repression: Cherry Plum Fruit, Pink Cherry, Original Innocence, Blue Delphinium, Child's Play, Honesty, Loving Me – Loving You, Disciple of the Heart, Pussy Willow, Celandine, Living the Dream, Passionate Life, The Rose, Red Poppy, Inner Fire, Heart Flow, *Self Worth (comb)*, *Self Expression (comb)*, *Take Time (comb)*

Resentment: Red Poppy, Pussy Willow, True Power, Goldenrod, Inner Fire, Phoenix Rebirth, Red Quince, Blue Delphinium, Heart Mother, With Love, Speedwell, Comfrey, Red Deadnettle, Cyclamen, *Forgiveness (comb)*, *Self Worth (comb)*, *Time Out (comb)*

S.A.D: Father Sun, Celandine, Green Alexanders, Stitchwort,

Seeing: Blue Salvia, One Being, Speedwell, Blue Delphinium, Reunion, Goldenrod, Lilac, Pussy Willow, Inner Fire, Rosebay Willowherb, *At One (comb)*

Sensitivity: Stitchwort, Speedwell, Peaceful Detachment, Pink Cherry, Red Clover, Divine Being, Physostegia, Heart Mother, Reunion, Rosebay Willowherb, *Light Heart Space (comb), Lighter Space (comb)*

Seriousness: Child's Play, Reunion, Living the Dream, Celandine, Golden Blessings, Passionate Life, *Passionate Life (comb)*

Shyness: Orange Wallflower, Goldenrod, Red Poppy, Inner Fire, Blue Delphinium, Physostegia, Honesty, Loving Me – Loving You, Red Deadnettle, Original Innocence, Heart Mother, Wild Cyclamen, Cyclamen, Crab Apple Fruit, Yellow Hyacinth, *Self Worth (comb), Self Expression (comb)*

Sleep: Bluebell Grove, Speedwell, Red Clover, Cyclamen, Heart Mother, Stitchwort, Letting Go, Grandmothers Arms, Pussy Willow, *Sleep Well (comb)*

Singing: Celandine, Blue Delphinium, Heart Flow, Physostegia, Loving me – Loving You, *Self Expression (comb)*

Sexuality: (see also Abuse) Red Gladiolus, Horse Chestnut Leaf Bud, Pure Love, Loving Me – Loving You, Pink Cherry, Pussy Willow, Yellow Hyacinth, Beauty in the Eye, Blue Delphinium, *Sexual Healing (comb), Make Love (comb)*

Shame: Original Innocence, Crab Apple Fruit, Honesty, Heart Flow, Red Quince, *Self Worth (comb)*

Shock: Crimean Snowdrop, Stitchwort, Red Clover, Letting Go, Divine Being, *Peace in a Storm (comb)*

Singing: Celandine, Blue Delphinium, Honesty, The Rose, Heart Flow, Loving Me – Loving You, *Self Expression (comb)*

Softening: Pink Cherry, Pussy Willow, Grandmothers Arms, Cyclamen, Yellow Hyacinth, Beauty in the Eye, Loving Me – Loving You, Speedwell, Heart Flow, Bluebell Grove, Child's Play, Lilac, *Time Out (comb)*

Space Clearing: Original Innocence, Crimean Snowdrop, Peaceful Detachment, Divine Being, *Lighter Space (comb)*

Spiritual Connection: At the Heart of Being, One Being, Speedwell, Sweet Pea, Rosebay Willowherb, Reunion, Bluebell Grove, *At One (comb)*

Stress/Pressure: Speedwell, Lilac, Pussy Willow, Grandmothers Arms, Cyclamen, Heart Mother, With Love, Physostegia, Living the Dream, Bluebell Grove, Child's Play, Disciple of the Heart, Comfrey, *Time Out (comb), At One (comb), Working Harmony (comb)*

Study/Learning: Lilac, Speedwell, Reunion, Comfrey, Disciple of the Heart, The Rose, *Working Harmony (comb)*

Time/Timelessness: Speedwell, Sky Blue Comfrey, Comfrey, At the Heart of Being, Pussy Willow, Lilac, Living the Dream, *Take Time (comb)*

Throat Chakra: Blue Delphinium, Celandine, Honesty, Heart Flow, The Rose, Physostegia, Red Quince, *Self Expression (comb)*

Transformation: Letting Go, Reunion, Living the Dream, Cherry Plum Fruit, Divine Being, Stitchwort, Original Innocence, Phoenix Rebirth, *Peace in a Storm (comb), Forgiveness (comb)*

Trust: Living the Dream, Pussy Willow, Goldenrod, Divine Being, At the Heart of Being, Pure Love, With Love, Disciple of the Heart, Wild Cyclamen, Sweet Pea, *Infinite Abundance (comb), Peace in a Storm (Comb)*

Twins/Twin souls: Reunion, Peaceful Detachment, One Being, At the Heart of Being

Victim Mentality: Red Poppy, Inner Fire, Physostegia, Goldenrod, True Power, Blue Delphinium, Violet, Red Quince, Red Deadnettle, Phoenix Rebirth, Divine Being, Sweet Hunza, Celandine, Crimean Snowdrop, Orange Wallflower, Living the Dream, Heart Mother, With Love, Sky Blue Comfrey, Wild Cyclamen, *Passionate Life (single essence and comb), Forgiveness (comb), Self Worth (comb)*

Vitality: Green Alexanders, Stitchwort, Divine Being, Passionate Life, Red Clover, Red Poppy, Celandine, Cyclamen, Bluebell Grove, Grandmothers Arms, Crab Apple Fruit, *Self Healing (comb), Passionate Life (comb)*

Vulnerability: Divine Being, Wild Cyclamen, Red Clover, Stitchwort, Letting Go, Passionate Life, Crimean Snowdrop, Red Poppy, Goldenrod, Physostegia, Blue Delphinium, Inner Fire, Reunion, Cherry Plum Fruit, Honesty, Heart Flow, Original Innocence, Father Sun, Green Alexanders, Crab Apple Fruit, *Passionate Life (comb), Peace in a Storm (comb), Light Heart Space (comb); Self Healing (comb), Self Worth (comb)*

Womanhood: Red Gladiolus, Pink Cherry, Heart Mother, Grandmothers Arms, Cyclamen, Loving Me – Loving You, Pussy Willow, With Love, Lilac, Speedwell, *Women's Balance (comb), True Beauty (comb)*

Women's Sexuality: Red Gladiolus, Loving Me – Loving You, Horse Chestnut Leaf Bud, Pure Love, Original Innocence, Crab Apple Fruit, Yellow Hyacinth, Beauty in the Eye, Pink Cherry, Blue Delphinium, Child's Play, Red Deadnettle, *Sexual Healing (comb), Make Love (comb)*

Worry: Red Clover, Stitchwort, Letting Go, Peaceful Detachment, Heart Mother, Divine Being, Crab Apple Fruit, Living the Dream, Crimean Snowdrop, Sky Blue Comfrey, *Peace in a Storm (comb), Light Heart Space (comb), Infinite Abundance (comb), Self Healing (comb)*

Acknowledgements

So many people have loved, supported, taught and inspired me over the years. It is not possible to name them all but somehow a part of each of them is in this book.

My love and gratitude goes firstly to those in spirit:
To my wonderful parents.
To my dearest friend Sally.
To Ivy Northage and Chan.
To the Sirius group – for being my 'family'- for sharing their wisdom, inspiration and understanding in co-creating these essences and their descriptions – and for walking beside me on my 'inside out', 'outside in' journey.
To the plants, the plant spirits, and the natural world.
To the animal spirits who have walked and flown with me, particularly the owls, wolves, eagles, butterflies and the dragonflies.

My love and gratitude to all those on this planet, who have shared the highs and lows of my journey with me – most especially:
To my husband and best friend, Mark, for walking beside me through thick and thin, and for sharing with me the last twenty three years.
To my wonderful shiny children: Jude, Dulcie, Beth and Gabriel.
To Jenny Turner – most wonderful friend and heart sister.
To my sister Belinda – for her loving support.
To Viv Williamson, Hannah Giffard, David Brittain, Paul Parolin, Steph Woods, Flic Price, Carol Rudd, Linda Heagerty, Linda Cartwright, Pat Staines, Peter Tadd, Don Dennis, Helen Johnson, David Gillett, Jacqui Beacon, Val Bullen, Tara Devi, and to Paul and Susan Tuttle and Raj, for their friendship, healing and inspiration.
To all my clients – for their teaching, and for the inspiration of their

courage.

To those people who don't know me, but whose work has inspired my work and understanding over the years:

To Brandon Bays – for her profoundly healing 'Journey' work (also for kindly agreeing to my reproducing the 'Camp Fire Process' in this book.

To Lyn Grabhorn – for her wonderful book 'Excuse Me, Your Life is Waiting'.

To Sam (White Buffalo Stands Alone) – for his medicine wheel stones and for the connection to the land, the spirits and the elders.

To David Carson – for his beautiful Medicine Cards – messages from spirit 'family'.

To Jani King and P'taah.

My gratitude and appreciation goes to those who have helped me so much in the production of this book and cards:

To Richard Osborne (Brightstar Creative.com) for creating such an inspiring book cover and for designing the boxes and flier – thank you for once again understanding my intention and my dream, and for taking so much care.

To Meraylah Allwood for her beautiful line drawings.

To Jenny Turner for her beautiful and profound images for the Living the Dream and Original Innocence cards.

To Graham Booker for all the care he put into designing and laying out the cards, for his beautiful design of the radiant pink heart, for the Child's Play card, for overcoming his horror of pink (!), and making me laugh so much.

To Kenny Millie – the ever-patient, laidback, typesetting genius.

To Steve Tolley at Carta Mundi for endless help with arranging the cards and packaging of the book and cards.

To all the crew at the printers – Mackays of Chatham.

To Paul and Danny and everyone at Hangar Press.

About the Author

Rose Titchiner is the mother of four children, two sons and two daughters, (aged between 29 and 9 years old). She lives in North-east Suffolk, with her husband Mark and their three younger children, at the house that has been their home for most of the last twenty-two years.

She loves hanging out with her family and friends, going for long walks, cycling, Canadian canoeing, crazy dancing, swimming in the sea, gardening, wearing nice clothes, photographing flowers, watching videos, eating ripe mangoes and reading exciting and magical children's books.

Apart from making the Light Heart Essences, Rose spends most of her time working as a flower essence therapist and healer, with both adults and children. She also runs courses and workshops on emotional and spiritual healing, and flower essences.

She is the co-author and publisher of the book 'New Vibrational Flower Essences of Britain & Ireland' (Waterlily Books 1997), a founder member, and full practitioner member of the BFVEA (British Flower & Vibrational Essences Association) and a member of the BFVEA Executive Committee. She is also a member of BAFEP (the British Asoociation of Flower Essence Producers), and a governor at her local primary school.

Suggested Reading List

Therapy
The Journey – *Brandon Bays*
Pure Bliss – *Gill Edwards*
What We May Be – *Piero Ferucci*
How Love Works – *Steve and Shaaron Biddulph*
Raising Boys – *Steve Biddulph*
You Can Heal Your Life – *Louise Hay*
The Indigo Children – *Lee Carroll & Jan Tober*
Excuse Me, Your Life is Waiting – *Lynn Grabhorn*
Working With Your Chakras – *Ruth White*
I'm Fine (Learning to Unblock Your Emotions) – *AndrewTresidder*
The Parents Book – *Ivan Sokolov & Deborah Hutton*
Anyone Can Dowse for Better Health – *Arthur Bailey*
Quantum Healing – *Deepak Chopra*
Perfect Health – *Deepak Chopra*
Ageless Body, Timeless Mind – *Deepak Chopra*
Cutting the Ties that Bind – *Phyllis Krystal*

Spiritual Healing/Enlightenment
P'taah, The Gift – *Jani King*
P'taah, Act of Faith – *Jani King*
P'taah, Transformation of the Species – *Jani King*
I come as a Brother – *Bartholemew*
Reflections of an Elder Brother – *Bartholemew*
From the Heart of a Gentle Brother – *Bartholemew*
Conversations with God – *Neale Donald Walsh*
The Awakening Letters – *Cynthia Sandys*
Journey Into Nature – *Michael J. Roads*

Messages from Water – *Masaru Emoto*
The Power of Now – *Eckhart Tolle*
On the Death of my Son – *Jasper Swain*

Divination
Medicine Cards – *Jamie Sams and David Carson*
How to Use the I Ching – *Stephen Karcher*
The Transformation Game – *(available from the Phoenix Bookshop, Findhorn, Scotland)*

Management Theory and New Science
Leadership and the New Science – *Margaret J. Wheatley*
A Simpler Way – *Myron Kellner-Rogers & Margaret J. Wheatley*
Appreciative Enquiry – *Jane Magruder Watkins and Bernard J. Mohr*
The Field – *Lynne McTaggart*

Connection to the Spirit in Nature/Shamanism
Animal Speak – *Ted Andrews*
Medicine Cards – *Jamie Sams and David Carson*
Buffalo Woman Comes Singing – *Brooke Medicine Eagle*
Shaman – *Susan Seddon Boulet*
The Healing Energies of Trees – *Patrice Bouchardon*
The Sacred Tree – *Glennie Kindred*
The Earth's Cycle of Celebration – *Glennie Kindred*

Guides to British Flora
Flora Brittanica – *Richard Mabey*
Plants With a Purpose – *Richard Mabey*
The Englishman's Flora – *Geoffrey Grigson*
Wild Flowers of Britain – *Roger Philips*
Wild Flowers of Britain & Northwest Europe – *Christopher Grey-Wilson*
Trees in Britain – *Roger Philips*
The Medicinal Flora of Britain and Northwestern Europe – *Julian Barker*
A Modern Herbal – *Mrs M. Grieve*
The New Holistic Herbal – *David Hoffman*
The Healing Spirit of Plants – *Clare Harvey & Amanda Cochrane*

Flower Essence Books
New Vibrational Flower Essences of Britain and Ireland – *Titchiner, Monk, Potter & Staines*
A Compendium of Flower Essences – *Harvey, Tadd & Dennis*
Flower Essences, An Illustrated Guide – *Carol Rudd*
Flower Essences & Relationships – *Martin J. Scott & Gael Mariani*
Bach Remedies & Other Flower Essences – *Vivien Williamson, with Dr Andrew Tresidder*
Bach Flower Therapy – *Mechthild Scheffer*
A Guide to the Bach Flower Remedies – *Julian Barnard*
Bach Flower Remedies For Animals – *Helen Graham & Gregory Vlamis*
The Bailey Flower Essences Handbook – *Arthur Bailey*
The Lazy Person's Guide to Emotional Healing: Using Flower Essences Successfully – *Andrew Tresidder*
Findhorn Flower Essences – *Marion Leigh*
Harebell Remedies Handbook – *Ellie Web*
Australian Bush Flowers – *Ian White*
Bush Flower Healing – *Ian White*
Energy Medicine – *Sabina Pettitt*
The Essence of Healing – *Steve Johnson*
Australian Flower Essences for the 21st Century – *Vasudeva and Kadambii Barnao*
The Healing Flowers – *Judy Griffin*
The Mana of Flowers – *Penny Medeiros*
Flower Essence Repertory – *Patricia Kaminski & Richard Katz*

Other Books that Have Inspired Me (including some Children's Books)
An Evil Cradling – *Brian Keenan*
Of Unknown Colour – *Winifred Nicholson*
The Woman of Wyrrd – *Lynn Andrews*
Wild Magic (and all other Tamora Pierce books!) – *Tamora Pierce*
The Little White Horse – *Elisabeth Goudge*
Harry Potter & the Chamber of Secrets (and all other Harry Potter books!) – *J.K. Rowling*

Useful Addresses

LIGHT HEART ESSENCES & ADDITIONAL COPIES OF THE HANDBOOK & CARDS ARE AVAILABLE FROM:

Light Heart Essences,
PO Box 35
Halesworth
IP19 0WL

Tel: +44 (0)1986 785216
e-mail: info@lightheartessences.co.uk
www.lightheartessences.co.uk

The complete range of Light Heart Essences, as well as various flower essence books, are available by mail-order from the above address. Orders can be purchased securely online, or by phone. For all trade enquiries, please e-mail us, or phone the above no. For enquiries about the essences, courses and workshops, or to book a phone consultation, please phone or e-mail us.

Also available from:
IFER (The International Flower Essence Repertoire)
The Living Tree
Milland
Liphook
Hants
GU30 7JS

Tel: +44 (0)1428 741572
Fax: +44 (0)1428 741679
e-mail: flower@atlas.co.uk

IFER supplies by mail-order, many of the world's finest flower essence ranges. They also offer a programme of flower essence courses throughout the year, with seminar teachers from around the world.

IFER also has a residential, educational base in Scotland:
IFER
Achamore House
Isle of Gigha
Argyll & Bute
Scotland
PA41 7AD

Tel: +44 (0)1583 505385
Fax: +44 (0)1583 505387
e-mail: gigha@atlas.co.uk
www.healingflowers.com

Achamore House is a large baronial mansion, set in 50 acres of magnificent gardens, on the Isle of Gigha in the Inner Hebrides. Home to IFER's Managing Director, Don Dennis, Achamore House runs an exciting schedule of residential flower essence courses, and seminars.

LIGHT HEART ESSENCES ARE ALSO AVAILABLE FROM:

Patterns of Light
www.patterns-of-light.com
e-mail: jennyPOL@aol.com

Patterns of Light is a wonderful emporium of inspiring gifts and flower essences. It has secure online purchasing.

IFEC (The International Flower Essence Centre)
PO Box 1144
Hartwell VIC, 3124
Melbourne,
Australia

www.floweressences.com.au
e-mail: info@floweressences.com.au
Tel: +61 (0)407 117 579 & +61 (3)98 897 176
Fax: +61 (0)398 897 688

IFEC supplies by mail-order, several of the world's finest flower essence ranges. They also produce a flower essence newsletter.

OTHER STORES AND WEBSITES SELLING FLOWER ESSENCES

Healthlines
www.healthlines.co.uk
e-mail: admin@healthlines.co.uk
Tel: +44 (0)1539 824099

A wonderful website, started and run by a group of homoeopaths, selling flower essences from international essence makers, homeopathic products, herbal remedies, books and many natural products. Secure online purchasing. They also organise flower essence workshops taught by international flower essence producers.

The Nutri Centre
7 Park Crescent
London W1B IBF

www.nutricentre.com
e-mail: enq@nutricentre.com
Tel: +44 (0)207 7436 5122

The Nutri Centre sells a comprehensive selection of international flower essences, and books on flower essence therapy (check out the books on their website), in addition to a wide range of natural products, supplements, herbs, homeopathic remedies, and more. You can shop in their London stores, or order products securely online.

Neals Yard Remedies
15 Neal's Yard
Covent Garden
London WC2H 9DP

www.nealsyardremedies.com
Tel: +44 (0)207 379 7222

Neals Yard remedies have stores throughout London, as well as throughout the rest of the UK, selling flower essences, vegetable glycerine, bottles and cream jars, lotion and cream bases, herbal remedies and dried herbs and tinctures, essential oils, natural cosmetics and cosmetic ingredients. You can buy from their shops, order products securely online, or by mail order. They also offer discounts for therapists.

The Cosmic Trader
76 Gillygate
York
YO31 7EQ

www.cosmictrader.com
Tel: +44 (0)1904 622706

Cosmic Trader sell a selection of international flower essences, as well as essential oils, tarot and divination cards and many other items. You can either visit their shop, or shop online from their secure website.

OTHER WONDERFUL FLOWER ESSENCE RANGES FROM BRITAIN & IRELAND:

Sun Essences & Sun Essences for Animals
Well Cottage
7 Church Road
Colby
Norwich
NR11 7AB

www.sunessence.co.uk
e-mail: enquiries@sunessence.co.uk
Tel: +44 (0)1263 723942

Essence makers Vivien Williamson and Jane Stephenson, make a beautiful set of Bach Flower Essences, wonderful combination essences for people, as well as some excellent combinations for animals, plus a range of single essences for therapists. Vivien Williamson is also the author of the book 'Bach Remedies and Other Flower Essences' (see Suggested Reading).

Indigo Essences
Dragonhold Stables
Newcastle
Co Wicklow
Ireland

www.indigoessences.com
e-mail: ann@indigoessences.com
Tel: +353 1 2011 671

Homoeopath Ann Callaghan, makes some amazing single and combination crystal essences, specifically for children. They are fun to use, as well as being very effective. Ann has designed her literature, bottles and shatterproof atomisers, so that children can choose for themselves the essences that they are most drawn to. Using the atomisers they can safely help themselves to their chosen flower essences whenever they feel the need.

Bailey Essences
7 Nelson Road
Ilkley
West Yorks
LS29 8HN

www.baileyessences.com
e-mail: office@baileyessences.com
Tel: +44 (0)1943 432012
Fax: +44 (0)1943 432011

Arthur Bailey has been making the Bailey Flower Essences 25 years. He makes a range of wonderful single essences as well as his renowned Composite Essences. He is also the author of the book 'Anyone Can Dowse for Better Health'.

Findhorn Flower Essences
Cullerne House
Findhorn
Moray
Scotland
IV36 3YY

www.findhornessences.com
e-mail: info@findhornessences.com
Tel: +44 (0)1309 690129
Fax; +44 (0)1309 691300

Marion Leigh makes the beautiful Findhorn Flower essences, which include both single and combination essences. She runs courses and workshops at Cullerne House, and has written an in-depth handbook for the Findhorn Essences. The Findhorn Essences can be purchased by mail-order from the above address, or can be purchased online from her secure website.

Harebell Remedies
81 Main Street
St John's Town of Dalry
Castle Douglas
Kircudbrightshire
DG7 3UP

Tel: +44 (0)1644 430607
e-mail: ellie@harebellremedies.co.uk

For many years, Ellie Web has been making her wonderful Scottish flower essences, and she now sells a range 64 single flower essences, plus combination flower essences, flower essence mists, and flower essence rollettes. Ellie also offers phone, postal, or e-mail flower essence consultations.

Green Man Essences
PO Box 6
Exminster
Exeter
EX6 8YE

Tel/Fax: +44 (0)1392 832005
e-mail: info@greenmanessences.com
www.greenmanessences.com

Simon and Sue Lilly make a range of over 100 tree flower essences from British and naturalised trees, as well as a series of combination essences for everyday use, and a range of shamanic power plant essences. Sue Lilly also makes the Sovereignty Essences ñ a set of composite essences linked to the yearly cycle of the earth. Simon and Sue have written three books on tree essences and working with tree spirits, and a number of books on colour, crystals and chakras. All of these, plus the essences are available by mail-order. Please phone or e-mail to order, or for any enquiries. Sue and Simon also run a number of correspondence and tutor led courses on flower essences, crystals, colour, and working with tree spirits.

OTHER USEFUL ADDRESSES:

The Homeopathic Supply Company
The Street
Bodham
Holt
Norfolk
NR25 6AD
www.homeopathicsupply.com
e-mail; orders@homeopathicsupply.com
Tel: +44 (0)1263 588788
fax: +44 (0)1263 588875

The Homeopathic Supply Company is run by Robert & Ann Barker, and provides a wonderful service supplying bottles, boxes, cases, homeopathic remedies, natural cosmetics and books. Fantastic efficient and helpful service. A company with its hand on its heart!

BFVEA (The British Flower & Vibrational Essences Association)
PO Box 33
Exmouth Devon
EX8 1YY

www.bfvea.com
e-mail: info@bfvea.com
Tel: 07985 512064

The BFVEA is an umbrella organisation representing all those interested in, or practising, flower essence therapy in the UK. It publishes a quarterly journal: 'Essence', a register of accredited Flower Essence therapists, and a list of BFVEA compliant practitioner training courses.

BAFEP (The British Association of Flower Essence Producers)
PO Box 100
Exminster
Exeter
Devon
EX6 8YT

www.bafep.com
e-mail: info@bafep.com
Tel: +44 (0)1392 832005

BAFEP was formed in 2000, by over 50 British flower essence producers. Linked to the BFVEA, its aims are to represent the interests of British flower essence producers, to set and maintain standards for flower essence production, to represent producers interests to other parties, and to be a consultative body for advice on flower essence production in Britain. It produces a quarterly newssheet for its members.

The Northwest Foundation for a Course in Miracles
PO Box 1490
Kingston WA 98346 – 1490
USA

e-mail: support@nwffacim.org
www.nwffacim.org

The NWFFACIM offers the Rajpur channelled talks, in the form of monthly workshops, weekly evening study groups, printed transcripts, and live web-casts and video-casts. All of the 'Raj' talks are channelled by Paul Tuttle. The work of the NWFFACIM, all workshops, and the distribution of the 'Raj' material, is supported entirely by voluntary donations.

The Journey (Brandon Bays)
PO Box 2
Cowbridge
CF71 7WN
UK

www.thejourney.com
e-mail: infoeurope@thejourney.com
Tel: +44 (0)1656 890400
Fax: +44 (0)1656 890182

For information about all of Brandon Bays courses and workshops, visit the website, or phone or e-mail for details. Books, cards, cds and audio tapes, can be purchased online from The Journey secure website.

Dowsing Chart

43	19	50	55
11	23	45	2
41	44	52	36
7	29	31	54
47	53	8	17
22	42	51	9
12	37	33	21

Dowsing Chart

15	49	56	3
1	14	32	48
18	25	5	40
10	46	4	16
20	38	26	13
35	28	6	24
30	34	27	39

Essence Page Index

Notes